Triumph and Tragedy

Triumph and Tragedy

The Inspiring Stories of Iowa Football Legends
Fred Becker, Jack Trice, Nile Kinnick and Johnny Bright

By
Mike Chapman

CULTURE HOUSE BOOKS

TRIUMPH AND TRAGEDY

A publication of Culture House Books – June 2010

Copyright – 2010 by Mike Chapman
All rights reserved.

No part of this book may be reproduced or transmitted in any form or by any means, electronic or mechanical, including photocopying, recording, or by any information storage and retrieval system now known or to be invented, without permission in writing from the publisher, except by a reviewer who wishes to quote brief passages in connection with a written review for inclusion in a
magazine, newspaper, or broadcast.

For information, address: Culture House Books
P.O. Box 293
Newton, Iowa 50208
641-791-3072

Library of Congress Cataloging-in-Publication Data
Chapman, Mike, 1943 -
    Triumph and Tragedy.

    1. Football – United States – Biography.
    2. Football – United States – History.
    3. United States – University – Football – History.

ISBN 978-0-9819484-2-3

PRINTED IN THE UNITED STATES of AMERICA

First Edition

Table of Contents

Foreword by Jim Zabel 1

Introduction 5

Chapter One: 13
    Fred Becker: *"The Fighting Spirit"*

Chapter Two: 45
    Jack Trice: *"Two Games, Enduring Fame"*

Chapter Three: 67
    Nile Kinnick: *"A Hero for the Ages"*

Chapter Four: 113
    Johnny Bright: *"Drake's Shining Star"*

Epilogue 153

Bibliography 159

"Show me a hero and I will write you a tragedy."

– F. Scott Fitzgerald

Acknowledgements

This book came about due to the support of many people. Foremost among them is Paul Morrison, the legendary sports information director at Drake University, who saw every game Johnny Bright played, as well as two of Nile Kinnick's games in 1939. At age 92, Paul is long retired but still has an office in the athletic complex and is an amazing resource due to his energy, enthusiasm and dedication to all Iowa sports. I am also indebted to Jim Zabel, another Iowa sports legend, for writing a terrific foreword and offering his support for this project. Others that have helped in various ways are Mike Reese of Atlas Media, Jim Walden, Bud Grant, Jack Jennett, Arlo Doughty, Judith Whipple of the U.S.S. Lexington Museum on the Bay staff, and the sports information offices at Drake University, Iowa State University and the University of Iowa. Also, a special thanks to my wife, Bev, who helped edit and proofread this book and travels the state with me as I give speeches about these four legendary Iowans.

Foreword

We need to honor our heroes, not only for what they accomplished in life but for the inspiration they provide us in death. Too often we know them only as names displayed on a stadium wall or as a statue fronting an athletic complex.

Here, Mike Chapman has taken four iconic figures from our past – all of whom made their marks on the gridirons of Iowa – and brought them back to life: walking, talking, breathing human beings, competing with full emotion through the pages of this book. They all had one thing in common – they gave so much of themselves that they finally gave their lives.

We need to know about them. They are important. What they did was important. More than that, they are fascinating.

Fred Becker was an All-American at Iowa as a sophomore in 1916, but he gave up his final two years of athletic competition to enlist in the Marines in World War I. He was killed in France in 1918. He was awarded France's top military honor, the Croix de Guerre, and the Belgian War Cross for bravery. Over 5,000 attended his funeral in Waterloo.

Jack Trice was a conference champion in track and field at Iowa State, and he was in the starting football lineup as a sophomore in 1923. He suffered critical injuries in his second game, against Minnesota, and died several days later, as thousands prayed for him outside of his hospital window. The Cyclones now play in Jack Trice Stadium.

I was editor-in-chief of the Daily Iowan student newspaper in Iowa City when Nile Kinnick was killed. It was devastating. I had interviewed him twice. I went to my typewriter and wrote a letter to President Hancher, urging the University to immediately name the stadium after Kinnick. Two days later, the president wrote me back. He agreed that Kinnick deserved to be honored, but said

"Many men will lose their lives in World War II" and that we should "wait until hostilities have ended" before making a decision. Of course, the stadium was named for Nile in 1972.

Sports Illustrated called Kinnick "The last true student-athlete," which emphasizes the real significance of his storied legacy.

I agree with Mike that Johnny Bright may have been the best football player the state of Iowa has ever seen. He led the nation in total offense three straight years. More than that, he was outstanding in basketball, track and field and was a champion softball pitcher. Bright received national notoriety over the famed "broken jaw" incident, suffered at Oklahoma A&M, but he went to Canada and became an all-pro player there for many years.

Johnny was a terrific person. I considered him a great friend. I delivered a eulogy at his funeral service in 1983.

Maybe the title "Triumph and Tragedy" should be reversed. Their deaths were tragic, but the memories they left us were triumphant.

— *Jim Zabel, April 28, 2010*

Introduction

"**S**how me a hero and I will write you a tragedy," said F. Scott Fitzgerald, the author of *The Great Gatsby* and one of America's most respected wordsmiths.

Tragedy has been defined in various ways throughout the ages, from Homer to Shakespeare to Hemingway. The way it is viewed is often dependant upon one's range of experiences and upbringing, including parenting and education.

The parade of history is filled with heroes and it is also, sadly, filled with tragedies. This book will look at the lives and careers of four of the most important athletes in the history of the State of Iowa, and try to determine if their lives were tragic, or if their lives were, in retrospect, a beacon of energy, strength and inspiration for those who follow.

The idea for this book came to me late one summer evening in 2008 when I was driving past the front entrance to East Waterloo High School. It's a majestic entrance, wide and spacious, with huge steps, a concrete balcony, and a flagpole in center front. I got out of my car and walked up to the balcony, memories of high school days from nearly five decades earlier racing through my mind.

As I turned to leave, I spotted a small, weatherworn plaque next to the flagpole. I walked up to it, peering intently, and saw the following inscription:

"In memoriam to the boys of this school who gave their lives for freedom's cause. Lieut. Fred H. Becker, '14, died July 18, 1918, at Chateau-Thierry. Pvt. Lynn E. Miller, died October 9, 1916, at Camp Dodge. – In appreciation, East High, Class of 1920."

I was puzzled as I pondered the meaning of the plaque and the two names on it. I had never noticed it when I was attending school there in the years 1959 through 1961. Also, I considered myself something of an Iowa sports historian, having covered University of Iowa athletics during the years I was assistant sports editor of the Iowa City newspaper, and, later, as sports editor of The Gazette in Cedar Rapids, Iowa's second largest newspaper. I remembered that Fred Becker was the Hawkeyes' very first All-American football player, but was it possible he had graduated from "my" own high school and I hadn't known it?

The next day I called Phil Haddy, the long serving sports information director at Iowa, and asked him what he knew about Fred Becker. Haddy responded that he was the first All-American football player in Hawkeye history and was killed in action in World War I. Beyond that, he knew nothing. He did not even know what city Becker was from.

Determined to learn if the Fred Becker mentioned on the East High plaque was the same man who had been Iowa's first sporting legend, I went to the Waterloo Public Library and began looking through microfilm of old newspapers. An amazing story began to unfold in front of my eyes.

The two Fred Beckers were one and the same! I had never realized that East Waterloo had produced not only a World War I hero, as I was to soon to discover, but the very first All-American athlete in any sport at the University of Iowa.

Eager to share this information with others that I thought would be interested, I began telling the story of Fred Becker. One of the first people I called was Murray Wier, the legendary Hawkeye basketball player who had been my history teacher at East High in 1959. Wier had stirred the imagination of Iowa fans all across the state with his dynamic style of play in the late 1940s, and in 1948 was a consensus first-team All-American. To this day, he is the only Iowa basketball player to lead the nation in scoring (1948).

Murray spent 38 years at East High, including 24 as basketball coach and 36 as athletic director. He walked up those steps many times through the decades, right past that plaque. When I got him on the phone and asked him if he knew who Fred Becker was, he responded that he was Iowa's first All-American. Then I asked him if he knew where Becker attended high school and had served valiantly in World War I, dying in the service of his country in heroic fashion.

Wier admitted he had not known anything about Fred Becker. When I told Wier that there was a plaque out in front honoring Becker, he was flabbergasted.

"I've seen that plaque and read it but I never associated him with the football player of that name," he said. "And I knew nothing about his service during World War I. This is a wonderful story that everyone should hear about."

East High's athletic director at the time of my great discovery was Mike Allen, who had been a standout athlete at East in the late 1960s and came back to serve as athletic director. Sitting in his office, I told him the Becker story and together we walked out in front and looked at the plaque. Allen was, like Wier, very surprised that he had not known the story, and was delighted to learn about East's famous, and long forgotten, graduate.

The same was true everywhere I went in Waterloo. No one knew the story. The American Legion Post 138 in Waterloo is named after Fred Becker and Carl Chapman, a West High graduate who also died in the war, but the people at the post were not aware that Becker had been an All-American football player at Iowa.

Tim Hurley, mayor at the time and a former football player at Columbus High School, was delighted when he heard about "the real" Fred Becker. "It's a wonderful story and one we need to get out and talk about," he said.

In January of 2009, my wife, Bev, and I, started a new magazine called *Iowa History Journal*, with the express purpose of telling these types of stories and keeping them alive. In promoting the magazine, I have traveled the state giving speeches to groups that want to know more Iowa history. I tell about Fred Becker, of course, and how that amazing story had been overlooked for decades. Becker was featured on the cover of the October 2009 issue, looking resplendent in his Marine uniform. The headline on the cover says "Fred Becker: His Incredible story of Athletics and Patriotism."

The very first issue of *Iowa History Journal* featured Nile Kinnick on the cover. It boasted the first of a three-part series telling who Nile Kinnick was and why he is still so relevant to Iowans yet today. The conclusion is that Kinnick, a superb scholar, a historian and a football hero who died in World War II, has set the bar for excellence for all Iowans who have the courage to dream big and work hard.

Nile Kinnick is widely regarded as the greatest athlete ever produced in the state of Iowa, though such icons as Bob Feller, Dan Gable and Frank Gotch certainly have their advocates. However, what Kinnick accomplished his senior year goes far beyond the narrow confines of any one sport, or any one season. In that respect, he may indeed outshine any other Iowa product, including Feller, Gable and Gotch. After all, he was voted the Associated Press Male Athlete of the Year in 1939, ahead of such professional standouts as Joe Louis, Joe DiMaggio and Byron Nelson, heroes of boxing, baseball and golf, respectively.

As glorious as were Kinnick's football days at the University of Iowa, he had the tragic misfortune to become one of the casualties of World War II, passing from the scene before his twenty-fifth birthday, and leaving behind the enormous tragedy of unfulfilled potential. There are those who feel, and with some merit, he may have risen to a position of leadership of the very highest rank, even President of the United States of America.

Inspired by the lives of Fred Becker and Nile Kinnick, I began to research the stories of Jack Trice and Johnny Bright. I wanted to know why Trice's life, cut short at a young age in 1923, was so important that Iowa State would name its football stadium for him, the only African-American so honored in the entire nation. The August 2009 issue of *Iowa History Journal* carried a long story on the Cyclone legend.

In 2006, Drake University named its football field after Johnny Bright, another African-American. Bright had been a sensational athlete during his college days in 1949, '50 and '51, but had suffered from a stunning incident in 1951 that had racial overtones. After a great career in pro football, Bright had moved on to become an icon in education when he died unexpectedly at age 53.

All four men are united in the fact they are Iowa icons that experienced tremendous triumphs and endured terrible tragedy.

Becker, Trice, Kinnick and Bright were four of the finest men to ever play college sports. Three of them have football stadiums in the state named after them, while the first of the foursome has an American Legion post dedicated to his memory. It is the goal of this book to reacquaint you with their stories, and to help perpetuate their memories for further generations.

It seems that they deserve at least that. And along the way, their stories may inspire others to reach down deep inside and pull out the potential for greatness that lurks inside of us all.

— Mike Chapman, May 15, 2010

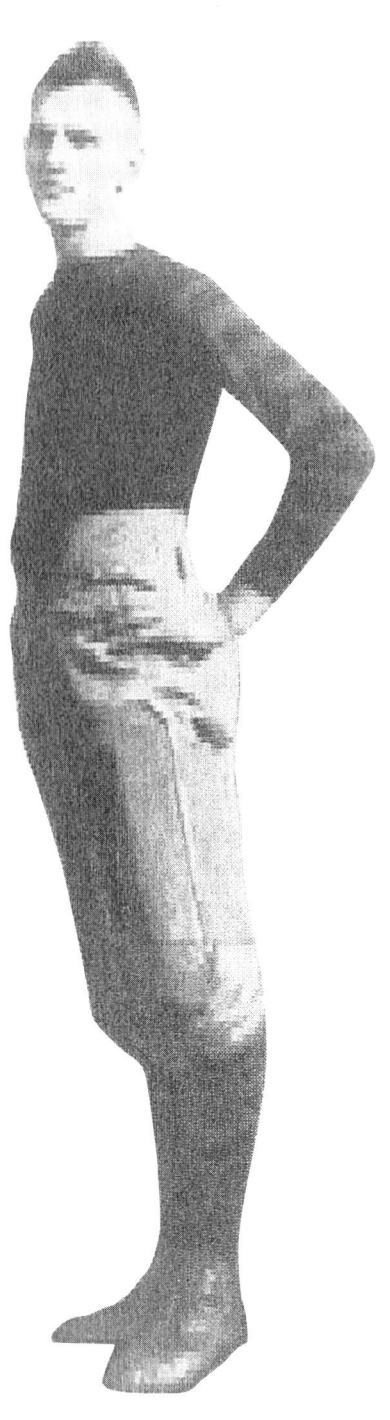

Fred Becker:

"The Fighting Spirit"

"Fred Becker was not only a Waterloo boy, he was more – he was a real Iowa boy. He was not only a typical son of our great state in the realm of physical prowess, where he excelled, but he was everything that a young man should be, morally and mentally, as well. He stood for everything that was wholesome, square, honorable, manly and American."

– Bill Atkinson, Speaker of the Iowa House

Fred Becker:

Iowa's First All-American

On a warm spring day, May 14, 1921, nearly five thousand people attended a funeral in Waterloo, Iowa. The previous day, hundreds had waited at the train station for the body to come from New Jersey. The day of the funeral, mourners packed the church, the overflow even covering the parking lot. That afternoon, they filled the local cemetery to the bursting point.

They came from all across the state to honor Fred Becker, who had given his life fighting as a doughboy in France during World War I. It was said to be the largest crowd ever assembled in the city on the Cedar River. The inspiration behind the turnout remains one of the most profound yet little-known stories in the annals of Iowa sports.

Fred H. Becker was born on November 6, 1895, in Waterloo, the third of three children raised by John and Marie. John was born in Albany, New York, and came to Iowa by covered wagon; Marie was born in Germany and came with her family to Iowa. The Becker family, which included sisters Hilda and Anna, lived in a solid, one-story house at 228 Newell Street, on the east side of the river. Ironically, it was just two blocks from the house on Adams Street where the five Sullivan brothers – who all perished on the same ship during World War II – were raised in the 1930s.

His early years offered scant evidence that Becker was going to be an exceptional athlete. Tall and gangly, he weighed just one hundred pounds by the time he entered ninth grade, dreaming of becoming a football star for East High School. Though thin in stature, Becker had one characteristic that seemed to stand out all through his athletic years: he was endowed with a fighting spirit, and it carried him to great success on the football field.

He first gained attention in sandlot games played on the patches of ground wherever enough boys could gather. Some of the organized games were held on the large lot by the Illinois Central Railroad offices, not far from the Becker home. It was in these rough-and-tumble games that he carved out a reputation as a tough customer. And it was his "fighting spirit" that set him apart from the other young athletes, said a local newspaper writer.

"Becker began playing football many years ago and was the star of the team from 'across the tracks,' when they clashed with Gordon Rath's team every Saturday morning on the Illinois Central grounds," began a story in the Waterloo Times Tribune paper of 1916, reporting on his success in college. "The lads from the north end did not have much of a team – but they did have Becker, who played the whole game for them and was the most sought-after player in the east side." He went on to become, said the paper, "East High's greatest fighter."

Becker enjoyed a highly successful high school career. Handsome and popular, he was involved in a variety of activities, ranging from football, basketball and track to several after-school clubs. He was elected vice president of the junior class, and was named sergeant at arms for the Zetagathian Society, a group of business students. He was also a member of the popular German Club. Little could he have imagined that he would one day give up his life fighting against Germany, the country where his mother had been born, and where his father's side of the family had originated!

Somewhere along the way, he picked up the nickname "Slats," which was fairly common for lean, rawboned young men of the era. Slats were the long, narrow pieces of hard wood underneath a bed that kept it together and allowed it to hold the weight of a person sleeping on the mattress. The nickname implied toughness of the sort admired by young boys.

The 1913 East High football team won three games and lost five. The annual school yearbook had the following to say about Becker: "Though not very large in diameter, 'Slats' made up in height what he lacked. Always in the game until the last minute and has a long reach, which could be depended upon to bring a man down. He played like a veteran and as he is only a junior he should shine on the field next fall."

Becker's final season at East High was very productive. The football team, called the Orange and Black, compiled a 5-1-1 record with Becker leading the way with his superb play in the line. East opened the season at Cedar Rapids and gained a 7-7 tie with a school that had been dominating East. "Every play showed that East High was fighting," reported the school newspaper. "In the latter part of the game, Fred Becker, our star center, was in practically every play that was pulled off by Cedar Rapids."

That winter, he was captain of the basketball team and the leading scorer in most games. By the time he graduated in the spring of 1915, Becker was being acknowledged as the best athlete in East High history.

Football became a club sport at the University of Iowa in 1872, but it was 17 more years until Iowa held its first official game, against Grinnell in 1889. The Hawkeyes initially played as an independent, and joined the Western Football Association in 1899. The conference was also called the Big Nine at the time, and didn't become known as the Big Ten until 1917 when the University of Michigan joined.

In 1913, the University of Iowa was paying its football coach, Jess Hawley, just $2,000 a year to lead the team. Hawley responded with the nation's top offensive unit. Though finishing just 5-2 on the season, Iowa led the nation in scoring with 310 points, and rolled up stunning wins over Northwestern (78-6) and Indiana (60-0).

Fred Becker arrived in Iowa City in the fall of 1915, when Hawley was starting what would become his final year as head coach. Freshmen were not eligible to play on the varsity so Becker spent the season laboring with the freshman team and learning the fundamentals of the game at the college level. Though not very thick, he was tall and lean and possessed of a competitive spirit that translated well onto the football field.

He often scrimmaged against the varsity, and that posed a problem for Hawley, it seems.

Becker's "work against the regular center (on the varsity) was so strong that Coach Hawley was at times forced to stop him from playing for fear that he would hurt the regular man," wrote a reporter for a Chicago paper.

Though the 1915 season wasn't much to brag about, a state record was set when a crowd of 11,000-plus showed up in Iowa City to see the Hawkeyes tangle with Iowa State. But a troubling fact disclosed at the end of the season caused hard feelings in football circles: many of the state's top high school athletes had left Iowa to play for other Midwestern schools. Five native Iowans were selected to the various all-conference teams, but the University of Iowa could claim just one!

The situation evoked a letter of concern from the Iowa Board in Control of Athletics to the president of the university. It declared that "This is the most important problem to be solved, and until it is solved by the alumni in the home towns making it their business to see that these boys attend their own state university, the University of Iowa cannot hope to have anything but mediocre teams."

Hawley had a successful investment career in Chicago and was therefore able to devote only limited time to coaching in Iowa City. Never more than a part-time coach at best, Hawley resigned after the 1915 season and the first fulltime coach was hired. His name was Howard Jones, and he was destined to become one of the greatest coaches in collegiate history.

Playing at Yale, Jones had been a star on a team that was undefeated for three straight years. During his tenure at Iowa, he would show that he had absorbed a tremendous amount of football knowledge at Yale, and in the following years.

".... a football dynasty had been born at Iowa with the signing of Howard Jones," wrote the authors of *75 Years With the Fighting Hawkeyes*. "Two consecutive Big Ten (called the Western Conference at the time) titles, a pair of unbeaten teams and a national championship – these would be only three of the hallmarks of Jones's teams during the next eight years." *(1)*

Jones was paid $4,500 for the first season, and immediately began to travel the state, looking for top candidates for his team. However, he already had one of the best players in Iowa history on campus, waiting in the wings – Fred Becker. Tall and lean, Becker had shown in high school and as a Hawkeye freshman that he was very aggressive on a football field and Jones couldn't wait to see him in action.

The Hawkeyes opened the 1916 season with a pair of traditional rivals, in non-conference games. The Hawks pounded Cornell and Grinnell by scores of 31-6 and 17-7, respectively, and claimed their third straight by whipping Purdue, 24-6. Becker's ferocious line play, on both offense and defense, was one of the main reasons the team had fared so well.

But reality showed up the next week when Iowa traveled north to take on national power Minnesota. The Gophers destroyed Iowa 67-0, and left the Iowa team reeling and humiliated. After losing 20-13 the following week to Northwestern at Evanston, Illinois, the Hawks took a two-game losing streak into Ames against a fired-up Iowa State team.

A record crowd of 15,000 was on hand to witness the showdown. It was to be Fred Becker's finest moment as a Hawkeye.

"The play of Becker, brilliant throughout, bulwarked Iowa's forward wall," said the authors of *75 Years with the Fighting Hawkeyes*. "With his team holding a narrow 17-13 lead in the fourth period against Ames, Becker crashed through to block two Cyclone punts, one giving the Hawkeyes an insurance safety and the other to keep the surging hosts deep in their own territory." *(2)*

Thanks in large part to Becker's play, Iowa won, 19-16.

Becker stood out on the field due to his tremendous play – and also because he wore no helmet most of the time. The leather helmets worn in that era were skimpy and could slide down over a player's eyes, and their use was optional. In the several photos that remain from the 1916 season, Becker is shown bare headed!

During the season, Becker established just as solid a reputation off the field as on. He joined the Kappa Sig fraternity and, judging by a story that appeared in a Waterloo paper, he was making his presence felt everywhere he went.

"Fred Becker, the former East High star who is playing center on the Iowa University varsity this year, is one of the most liked men on the campus of Iowa

City. Every magazine and newspaper which is published by the university town has spoken very highly of the Waterloo boy's showing and has commented on his likeable character."

His competitive spirit was mentioned prominently as the paper added that "he is on the high road to football fame. With only 166 pounds to back him up, he has made the team in his sophomore year thru (sic) sheer fight and ability."

Following the victory over Iowa State, the Hawkeyes closed out the season with a 34-17 loss to Nebraska. Though the team was just 4-3 for the season, the accolades began to roll in for the toughest Hawkeye. Becker was selected to the All-Western Conference team by several periodicals, including Collier's Weekly, Columbus (Ohio) Dispatch, Chicago Herald, Chicago Daily News and Ohio State Journal. An article in an Iowa newspaper summed it up this way:

"The honors came to the Waterloo boy because of his fighting qualities, which have manifested themselves from the time Becker first began playing the gridiron sport. This is the first time that a local football player has been chosen on an all-conference team, which makes it all the sweeter for him."

The highlight came when Becker was given a spot in the line on the All-America team chosen by Walter Eckersall, the foremost football writer of the era. That honor made him the first All-America athlete at the University of Iowa, in any sport!

"No matter where he was placed, his work was a feature," Eckersall wrote in the article announcing his team. "He was strong and powerful and quick to size up the attack of his opponents. He seldom failed to open holes for the backs and was on top of the play all year."

Eckersall added that Becker was "unparalleled in Iowa football annals," and he still had two more seasons ahead of him. No previous Hawkeye player had achieved such stardom on the national scene, and at such a young age.

The future for Iowa football and Fred Becker looked very bright. But while much of America was reveling in the exploits of its college football heroes, an extremely grave situation was developing in Europe. On June 28, 1914, while Becker was attending classes at East High School in Waterloo, Archduke Franz Ferdinand, heir to the Austro-Hungarian throne, was assassinated by a Bosnian

Serb. When Ferdinand's country responded by attacking Serbia, all hell broke loose.

Both countries had tight alliances with other European nations and within a month most of the continent was at war. The two main protagonists were the Entente Powers (consisting of France, Britain, Russia and other lesser forces) and the Central Powers (Germany, Austria-Hungary, the huge Ottoman Empire and Bulgaria). Italy joined the Entente in 1915, but the United States tried desperately to remain neutral. President Woodrow Wilson felt that runaway militarism was largely responsible for the war, and yet sided with Great Britain and France. He hoped the League of Nations would be able to broker a peace.

Former President Teddy Roosevelt led the American charge for entering the war and was beating the drums relentlessly. Wilson was able to hold the line until a telegram from Germany to Mexico was intercepted and translated. It showed that the Germans had tried to entice Mexico into joining the Central Powers, promising that in the event of the defeat of the United States, Mexico would receive as a reward the states of Arizona, New Mexico and Texas.

The sinking of seven U.S. Merchant Marine ships by German submarines was the final act that pushed America over the edge. On April 6, 1917, Congress declared war. Though America had a small army at the time, it initiated a draft and by the summer it was sending nearly 10,000 troops a day to France!

Like most other college students across the land, Becker certainly was aware of the tensions that were taking places overseas during the late fall and winter. And when war was officially declared by the United States, Becker answered the call. No doubt fueled by that fighting spirit that so many had seen in years previous, he left school and enlisted on March 16, 1917. His decision must have had a demoralizing effect on Coach Jones and thousands of Iowa football fans, even if they could understand his motives and patriotism.

"…. before the United States became involved in the European war, the football outlook for the season of 1917 was very encouraging," wrote Jones in *The Iowa Alumnus* journal. He added that "at the present time, it is difficult to line up the men who will return on account of the national conditions…."

"Football held a position of secondary importance in the fall of 1918 when the western front thundered with some of the mightiest battles of World War I," wrote the authors of *75 Years With The Fighting Hawkeyes*. "Gone from the college campuses of Iowa and other states were most of the rugged athletes of previous years." *(3)*

In May of 1917, Iowa's athletic director, Nelson Kellogg, left for Fort Snelling in Minneapolis to begin his military service. Howard Jones was appointed as his successor, and the task of holding two jobs must have taken a toll. Even Grinnell College was able to beat Iowa that fall, posting a 10-0 triumph in what was to be the last game ever played between the two schools. The rivalry had started in 1889 and held the distinction of being the first college football game ever played west of the Mississippi River. Iowa closed out the series with an 11-5-1 edge on the Tigers.

That summer, Becker also undertook his infantry training at Fort Snelling, and was commissioned a second lieutenant on August 15. He came back to Waterloo for a brief visit, seeing family and friends for what would be the last time. He departed on August 27 for the long voyage overseas. He arrived in France on October 1, 1917, and was sent to advanced officer's training. Though he was in the regular Army, he was transferred to the Marines Corps.

A story in the Waterloo paper told of the impact he made on those around him in training and in war: "During Becker's course of training at Fort Snelling and since his transfer to active duty in France, he has won the praise of the officers with whom he was associated. He was absolutely fearless on the football field and carried this same spirit into his duties on the battlefield."

The main war battleground in Europe was called the Western Front, a 475-mile long line between France and Germany. The other main battle area, the Eastern Front, separated Germany from Russia. Trench warfare was the main style of fighting that characterized the early stages of the war. The invention of weapons like the machine gun and flamethrowers made the crossing of open ground extremely dangerous, and deep trenches became the best means of protection.

One of the most famous novels of the 20th century, *All Quiet on The Western Front*, told in horrific detail what trench warfare was like along the main battle lines in France. Author Erich Maria Remarque had been a German soldier during the war, and had witnessed it first-hand, up close and personal. The book was a sensation. It was published in 1929 and within a year and a half had sold over two and a half million copies in 25 languages. It was made into a film in 1930, and won the Academy Award as best picture of the year.

The book's main character is a young German soldier named Paul Blaumer. Through his eyes and emotions, the reader experiences the devastating impact of war and the death of his comrades in a style that has made the novel a classic anti-war book. It is a story that sheds light on what Fred Becker experienced when he left the security and comfort of Iowa to become a part of "The War To End All Wars."

Blaumer understands the transition that must be made from the world of order and reason back home to the reality of war. Becker faced the same problems as he adjusted from the football fields of the Midwest to the battlefields of Europe.

"The idea of authority, which (the teachers back home) represented, was associated in our minds with a greater insight and a greater wisdom," said Blaumer in the book. "But the first death that we saw shattered this belief. We had to recognize that our generation was more to be trusted than theirs. They surpassed us only in phrases and cleverness.

"The first bombardment showed us our mistake, and under it the world as they taught it to us broke into pieces. While they continued to write and talk, we saw the wounded and the dying. While they taught that duty to one's country is the greatest thing, we already knew that death throes are stronger.

"We loved our country as much as they; we went courageously into every action; but also we distinguished the false from the true, we had suddenly learned to see. And we saw that there was nothing of their world left. We were all at once terribly alone; and alone we must see it through." *(4)*

The book offers a shattering depiction of war's reality settling into the psyche of young men …. young men with the hopes and dreams of an entire life ahead of them, but always on the brink of extinction. Surely every soldier, on either side of the Western Front, came face to face with the devastating possibilities before them. There were no guarantees of anything except sleepless nights of wondering and waiting. The terrors were everywhere and multi-faceted – rats slinking into the trenches searching for food, the lack of clean drinking water, lice-infested clothing, the incessant pounding of shells exploding all around, the screams of dying men and dying horses, and the long deathly quiets, when men went mad. Yes, there was madness in the trenches and along the Western Front.

Trench foot was another serious result of the War to End All Wars. Standing for hours in trenches filled with water presented a terrible problem. The wet, cold and unsanitary conditions led to swelling of the feet; the toes would turn colors, and either gangrene or amputation was often the result.

The days dragged on, and on, and on ….

"How long has it been?" asked an emotionally drained Blaumer at one point. "Weeks – months – years? Only days. We see time pass in the colorless faces of the dying, we cram food into us, we run, we throw, we shoot, we kill, we lie about, we are feeble and spent, and nothing supports us but the knowledge that there are still feebler, still more spent, still more helpless ones there who, with staring eyes, look upon us as gods that escape death many times." *(5)*

That was the world of Fred Becker in the summer of 1918, so far removed from the idyllic days of Waterloo and Iowa City. The war was raging on land and in the air. The arrival of fresh American troops boosted morale considerably among the Allied troops. One British nurse even went so far as to say that the tall, ramrod straight Americans looked almost like mythological heroes when they arrived. Another account said the Americans were itching to fight to such a degree that they often went tearing cross the open ground without regard to the consequences, and many were cut down quickly by machine gun fire.

Several months after Becker's arrival in France, Manfred Albrecht Freiherr von Rickthofen, was killed. Better known as The Red Baron, the German pilot was already the most famous flying ace of all time when he was shot down on the morning of April 21, 1918, along the Somme River. Undoubtedly, Becker and most other American troops would have known of the death of the Red Baron, whose fame was such that he was given an honorable burial by the Australian airmen who fought against him. Like most casualties of the war, von Richthofen was a young man – just a few days shy of his twenty-eighth birthday!

In 1916, Fred Becker became the first All-America athlete at the University of Iowa, in any sport.

Class Officers

Ray Berry, President
Carrie McFarlane, Vice President
Fred Becker, Secretary
Lora Bonsall, Treasurer

In this picture from the 1914 East High School yearbook, Fred Becker (second from right) is listed as one of the junior class officers.

When Fred Becker played for the Hawkeyes, games were held at the old Iowa Field located on the east side of the Iowa River, near where the current library sits.

In this rare photo from the 1916 season, Fred Becker (center, without helmet) is seen in action for Iowa against the University of Nebraska
(Photos courtesy of University of Iowa Athletic Department).

This advertisement is from a magazine dated June 20, 1918, and shows a Marine fighting in France during World War I. Fred Becker was a Marine officer in France at the very same time and could have been the soldier this portrait was modeled on. Lt. Fred Becker was killed on July 18, 1918, just 28 days after this ad appeared.

Funeral services for Lt. Fred Becker were held at Grace Methodist Episcopal Church (above) on May 14, 1921. The church, one of the largest in Waterloo, was filled to capacity and the overflow spilled into the parking lot.

Fred Becker is buried in a circle of 18 World War I veterans in Fairview Cemetery in Waterloo. His grave is third from the left in front. An estimated 5,000 persons attended the funeral on May 14, 1921.

But death was all around the soldiers and airmen on both sides of the trenches. During the lulls and quiet moments, Becker must have dreamed of those peaceful streets in his old Waterloo neighborhood, of boys and girls walking home from schools, of laughter in the backyards – and of autumn football Saturdays in Iowa City. But only in brief respites; by pure necessity, his main thoughts must have centered on survival, and wondering if he would ever see home again.

Like all other soldiers in wartime, Becker was alone; there were no Hawkeye teammates to help him on this field of combat. Surrounded by other doughboys on the front lines, every soldier was, as Blaumer said, "terribly alone …." and alone they must see it through.

The word "enemy" no longer referred to fellow college students playing an intense game for institutional pride and state bragging rights, but a fierce, unrelenting battle for one's survival. Blaumer's haunting words still echo across the ocean from the trenches of World War I.

July of 1918 was a terrible month. Remarque stresses that fact in poignant form near the end of his great work. There were in July, he reports, rumors of an armistice and with such talk, incredible hopes that it will all soon end:

"The summer of 1918 is the most bloody and the most terrible …. never was so much silently suffered in the moment when we depart again for the frontline …. never was life in the line more bitter and more full of horror than in the hours of the bombardment, when the blanched faces lie in the dirt. And the hands clutch at the one thought: No! No! Not now at the last moment! …. breath of hope that sweeps over the scored fields, raging fever of impatience, of disappointment, of the most agonizing terror of death, insensate question: Why? Why do they not make an end?" *(6)*

It was that same terrible summer that Remarque wrote about so dramatically that brought down Fred Becker.

"Ground combat is the worst experience a human being can have," said Colonel Oliver North on C-Span's Book Talk, talking about his new book, *American Heroes*. It was the day before Memorial Day. North's words have rung true for thousands of years, dating back to the Trojan War and beyond. They would prove to be the case for thousands of American combat troops sent to France to fight along the Western Front. *(7)*

On June 23, with less than a month to live, Becker wrote to his parents in Waterloo, telling them about the war and of an injury he had received a few days earlier. He had been struck in the left shoulder by shrapnel from a high explosive shell, but seemed to be recovering. He wrote that his company had been under heavy fire for over two hours at the time he was injured, and added he was anxious to return to battle.

"Everyone wants to get into action and all feel slighted when they are not engaged in combat when there is important work to be done," he wrote in his letter.

The last major offensive launched by the Germans on the Western Front was called the Battle of Reims, and also the Second Battle of the Marne. It took place at the Marne River, near Paris. The Germans were marching toward Paris, which terrified the city's citizens and caused a mass evacuation.

The Battle of Reims began on July 15, 1918, and lasted until August 5. The Allied casualties were stunning: 125,000 men were killed, including 95,000 from France, 13,000 from Britain and 12,000 Americans!

Three days after the battle began, the Allies stopped the Germans with ferocious fighting. Early on the morning of July 18, Ferdinand Foch of France, the Allied Supreme Commander, decided it was time to attack the stalled Germans. Eight large American Divisions, under General John J. "Black Jack" Pershing, teamed up with 24 French divisions for a furious counter-attack. Becker was fighting with the 5th Regiment of the United States Marine Corps.

On that day, the former Hawkeye All-American displayed the valor that would earn him everlasting glory in America's military annals. With his platoon pinned down by a German machine gun nest, Becker moved forward and took out the nest. The exact details are lost in the mists of time, but according to information sent from the Marines, his action was crucial in "preventing the death or injury of many men in his command."

The Marine Corps report continued: ".... his self-sacrificing courage permitted his platoon to advance, but as he completed the performance of this noble work, he himself was killed." *(8)*

The following account of the action appeared in the Waterloo paper.

"The fighting was at its height around Chateau-Thierry on the morning of July 18. Continued hammering by the American forces, which had been thrown into the fight at this point to stop the German advance on Paris, had not only stopped the onrush of the enemy, but had been successful in turning them back in the direction of Bellam Woods. The Americans were on the offensive in the entire section, the Germans protecting their rear through machine gun nests.

"Lt. Becker was killed while leading his men in advance on one of the enemy positions, being struck by a bullet. He was buried by his comrades in an open field on the south slope on the long hill east of Chateau-Thierry, and his grave marked with his rifle and a wooden cross."

Fred Becker paid the ultimate price for his country on July 18, 1918, nearly four thousand miles from home, some 18 months after earning All-American honors on the football fields of the Midwest. Two days later, the Germans began a retreat. The engagement in which Becker fell is called the Battle of Chateau-Thierry, named for a city 56 miles northeast of Paris.

"The allied forces had managed to keep their plans a secret, and their attack at 4:45 in the morning took the Germans by surprise when the troops went over the top," reported Wikipedia. They had charged "without a preparatory artillery bombardment, but instead followed closely behind a rolling barrage which began with great synchronized precision."

Some details of Becker's death came from a fellow officer, Lt. John D. Clark, who sent a letter to Fred's parents. He told them that Fred was found on the battlefield in advance of his comrades, "indicating that he was leading them in the fight." Fred had been shot in the throat and Clark added that he probably died instantaneously.

Less than three months after Becker's death, a sergeant from a poor family in the backwoods of Tennessee became a national hero when he led an attack on another German machine gun nest. Alvin Cullum York was a mere corporal when his 17-man unit slipped behind enemy lines and captured a large group of Germans. Suddenly, nine soldiers from his unit were cut down by another machine gun nest, leaving York in charge of the remaining seven.

York was awarded the Medal of Honor for his incredible actions, which included leading his shrunken command of battered troops in the killing of 25 of the enemy and capturing 132 others. His description of the battle against the machine guns provides a sense of what Becker must have faced.

"And those machine guns were spitting fire and cutting down the undergrowth all around me something awful. And the Germans were yelling orders. You never heard such a racket in all of your life. I didn't have time to dodge behind a tree or dive into the brush.

"As soon as the machine guns opened fire on me, I began to exchange shots with them. There were over thirty of them in continuous action, and all I could do was touch the Germans off as fast as I could. I was sharp shooting …. all the time I kept yelling at them (the Germans) to come down. I didn't want to kill any more than I had to. But it was they or I. And I was giving them the best I had." *(9)*

York was promoted and given numerous awards for his actions. On November 11, 1921, he was selected as a pallbearer at the Tomb of the Unknown Soldier when it was dedicated. The tomb is decorated with six carved wreaths which represent the six major battles of World War I – including Chateau-Thierry, where Lt. Fred Becker gave his life.

The soldier from Tennessee became a part of American folklore when Gary Cooper, one of the biggest stars in Hollywood history, portrayed him in the classic 1941 movie "Sergeant York," and won the Academy Award as best actor.

Today, the biggest hero of World War I is honored in numerous ways, including the Sergeant York Historic Trial in the Argonne area of France where he fought so valiantly. And even a football trophy competed for between Tennessee colleges Austin Peay, Tennessee State and Tennessee Tech is called the Alvin C. York Trophy.

York is one of the few who came home and became a hero. Many other young men simply ceased to exist …. or lost their youth completely.

"We are not youth any longer," wrote Remarque in *All Quiet on the Western Front*. "We don't want to take the world by storm. We are fleeing. We fly from ourselves. From our life. We were eighteen and had begun to love life and the world; and we had to shoot it to pieces. The first bomb, the first explosion, burst in our hearts. We were cut out from activity, from striving, from progress. We believe in such things no longer; we believe in the war." *(10)*

Remarque's writings may help explain why Becker charged the second machine gun nest on that fateful day. Perhaps he, too, had come to believe in the war at that point above all else. Or did he remember that day in Ames when he bolted through the Iowa State defense twice to block punts in such dramatic fashion, earning the cheers of the Hawkeye faithful and the accolades from Walter Eckersall.

Did the young doughboy from Waterloo, Iowa, make the fatal mistake of thinking it was all still a game, even of the most extreme design? We will never know the truth, but once again an answer of some sort comes from the pages of *All Quiet on the Western Front*. Near the end, the German soldiers have found a little cellar in an abandoned house to use as a place to rest.

"This is an opportunity not only to stretch one's legs, but to stretch one's soul also," writes Remarque. "We make the best of such opportunities. The war is too desperate to allow us to be sentimental for long. That is only possible so long as things are not going too badly. After all, we cannot afford to be anything but matter-of-fact. So matter-of-fact, indeed, that I often shudder when a thought from the days before the war comes momentarily into my head. But it does not stay long." *(11)*

To dwell on the past in such dire circumstances would be to invite disaster, and Becker was too smart for that, it would seem. His death appears to be born out of two factors – an intense belief in himself and in his "fighting spirit."

For his wartime actions, Fred Becker was awarded the American Distinguished Service Cross, second only to the Congressional Medal of Honor among this nation's highest wartime honors. He also received the Belgian War Cross and the Croix de Guerre, the top award France can bestow for battlefield heroism. He is the most decorated war-time soldier in Waterloo history, according to Brigadier General (retired) Evan Hultman, himself a top athlete at East High and a Hawkeye letterman.

The fact that Iowa's first All-American football player was awarded the Croix de Guerre takes on special meaning when one remembers that Nile Kinnick,

Iowa's most lionized player, referred to the French award on December 6, 1939, when accepting the Heisman Trophy in a stirring speech at the New York Athletic Club. Said Kinnick:

"Finally, if you will permit me, I'd like to make a comment which in my mind is indicative, perhaps, of the greater significance of football and sports emphasis in general in this country, and that is, I thank God that I was warring on the gridirons of the Midwest and not on the battlefields of Europe. I can speak confidently and positively that the players of this country would much more, much rather struggle and fight to win the Heisman Trophy than the Croix de Guerre."

One can only wonder if Nile Kinnick knew of Fred Becker's sacrifice on behalf of his nation when he compared college football to the war raging in Europe.

Becker wasn't the only Iowa athlete to enroll in the Armed Services of the United States and fight in France. Or to die there. Frank Grubb, a native of Panora and Becker's teammate on the 1916 Iowa football team, was killed in battle that same summer. He was found dead on the Western Front in a hole made by a shell. In his hand was a crumpled note that read: "They got me, but I got three of them first." Grubb lettered in football and track in both 1915 and 1916 and also wrestled for the Hawkeyes.

Harrison Cummins McHenry was a star in football and track at Drake and graduated from its law school in 1914. He came from a distinguished Des Moines family and had been valedictorian of his senior class at Des Moines West High School. His maternal uncle, Albert B. Cummins, was governor of Iowa. McHenry was serving as an officer in the Iowa National Guard when he was killed by a German military bombardment on March 5, 1918 – four months before Fred Becker lost his life. Captain McHenry was the first Iowa officer killed in the war.

Earl Caddock lived in the small farming community of Anita as a youth and won three national wrestling titles as an amateur. He then captured the world professional heavyweight championship in 1917, when the pro sport was still legitimate. Known as "The Man of A Thousand Holds," Caddock was a clean-cut, handsome and articulate athlete who was selling out arenas all across the Midwest. Like Becker, Caddock felt a duty to enlist.

He underwent training at Camp Dodge in Des Moines and turned down an officer's rank when it was offered, saying he preferred to be one of the regulars. Like Becker, he saw fierce action in France and even suffered from lung damage during a mustard gas attack. But, unlike Becker, he came home and his life continued.

The impact from Word War I was overwhelming and long-lasting. On both sides, it is estimated that a total of 20 million perished, including military personnel and civilians. The Great War broke up the fabled Ottoman and Austro-Hungarian empires and changed the landscape of Europe and the Middle East. Tragically, it laid the foundation for another world war just two decades later.

The war also swept away millions of young people, depriving the world of untold skills and leadership for decades to come. It is estimated that America suffered 117,465 deaths in World War I, and another 205,690 were wounded. That does not, of course, include those suffering from shell shock, or post-traumatic stress disorder as it is now called.

"The tragedy of war isn't to the people who start the war, it's to the 18- and 19-year-olds who have to fight the war," said historian and author William Fortschen, while promoting the book *Days of Infamy*, co-written with Newt Gingrich, former Speaker of the House. *(12)*

Indeed it is.

Fred Becker was buried on the battlefield where he fell, but his body did not remain in France. The War Department was anxious to bring home as many soldiers as possible, and on May 7, 1921, the body of the former Hawkeye hero arrived in Hoboken, New Jersey. It was transported by train to Waterloo, where it arrived on May 13.

A large crowd of family and friends were at the train station to see the flag-draped casket removed, and taken to the O'Keefe & Towne Funeral Home. An honor guard was posted around the clock, until the day of the funeral. The event was front page news in the Waterloo Evening Courier, under a headline, "Thousands join in last tribute to Lieut. Becker."

The gathering at stately Grace Methodist Episcopal Church was huge, and the occasion very solemn. Then the body was taken to the cemetery, where an even larger gathering was present.

"While 5,000 persons stood with bowed heads, the mortal remains of Lieut. Fred H. Becker were consigned to their last resting place in the soldiers plot in Fairview Cemetery yesterday afternoon," began the story. Following brief speeches and the volleys of shots over the grave, taps were played.

"Thus was taken the last step in the transplanting of the remains of the American boy, brave and true, who made the supreme sacrifice for his country, from the poppy fields of France to a sunny slope in beautiful Fairview, there to rest under the lilies and the roses.

"Never before in the history of Waterloo has there been such an outpouring of people to a funeral. Grace Methodist Episcopal Church, one of the largest in the city, was filled to capacity nearly an hour before the time set for the services to begin. Two thousand persons crowded into the edifice and as many more were unable to obtain entrance. The steps, the churchyard and the adjoining sidewalks were packed."

Reverend Henry Mueller was the main speaker at the cemetery. He told the vast crowd that "to leave home and loved ones, to give up for the time being the pursuance of a cherished ambition – a medical course in a university – to separate from friends and assume the duties of a soldier, these are the things that mean more than bravery; they bespeak the very highest form of patriotism."

Becker had been planning a career in medicine, and had hopes of becoming a surgeon. One high school teacher had compared his dedication to that of the famous Mayo brothers in Rochester, Minnesota.

In the November 11, 1956, edition of the Waterloo Sunday Courier, photos of Lt. Becker and Lt. Carl Chapman graced the front page. The caption read that they were the "first Waterloo men to be killed in World War I" and that they would be honored at Veterans Day Ceremonies at Soldiers and Sailors Park.

In the accompanying article, Courier reporter Francis Veach wrote: "Then there was Carl Chapman, one of the first airmen from Iowa, and Fred Becker, one of the first from Iowa with the Marine Corps who supported the Rainbow Division at Chateau-Thierry. Both Chapman and Becker were killed in action. Chapman had been a quarterback on the West High football team. Becker was an all-state football player for East High.

"This was when the great adventure turned to reality and the boys from Waterloo said goodbye to youth – and the gray memories began."

"Fred Becker and Carl Chapman were cross-town rivals and gridiron opponents," wrote Pat Kinney in the May 30, 2004, 150-year anniversary issue of the Waterloo Courier. "They became brothers in arms and decorated heroes of two nations. They both entered World War I. Becker, a U.S. Marine Corps lieutenant, was killed in action taking out a German machine gun nest near Vierzon, France.

"Chapman, a fighter pilot, was shot down in aerial combat over Toul, France. Both won the U.S. Distinguished Service Cross and the French Croix de Guerre." *(13)*

They were not the only area soldiers to see action overseas during that tumultuous time. A group of soldiers comprised of African-Americans from Waterloo served in the war. They received "a rousing sendoff with a parade headed by the mayor, city council and other public officials, and attended by most of the black community," wrote Kinney.

Shortly after Becker's death, Corliss Shirley of Waterloo found himself in a terrible situation in the same area. He was among 600 doughboys captured by German soldiers on October 2, 1918. They were surrounded by enemy forces in the Argonne Forest, in a portion called the Charleveaux Ravine. Shirley's group held out for nearly a week until, faced with starvation, they were forced to surrender. The American unit became known as the "Lost Battalion." Of the 600-plus captured, less than 200 survived the ordeal.

Unlike Becker, Shirley returned to his hometown and lived in Waterloo until dying in 1990. Shirley was 98 at the time of his death, outliving Becker by nearly 75 years!

"Becker and Chapman died to make this world a better place in which to live," said Ralph A. McGinnis, state commander of the American Legion, in ceremonies in 1927. "If Becker and Chapman would have lived, they today would be among the leaders of this country in all programs of civic advancement."

Many World War I veterans returned to live for many decades. An article carried over the Associated Press told of a Toledo, Ohio, man who died in late 2007: "J. Russell Coffey, the oldest known surviving veteran of World War I has died. The retired teacher, one of only three U.S. veterans from the War to End All Wars, was 109.

"More than 4.7 million Americans joined the military from 1917-1918. Coffey never saw combat because he was still in basic training when the war ended. Coffey had enlisted in the Army while he was a student at Ohio State University in October, 1918, a month before the Allied powers and Germany signed a cease-fire agreement."

On March 7, 1939, John and Marie Becker celebrated their 50th wedding anniversary in Waterloo. It was nearly 21 years after the loss of their only son in France and just several months before the most famous football player in Iowa history, Nile Kinnick, would begin his final season.

On March 30, 1921, American Legion Post 138 in Waterloo was named in honor of Becker and Chapman. Among the bits of memorabilia currently stored at the post is a loose-leaf notebook with the name Becker etched in large letters on the cover. It is 36 pages long, and contains Becker's handwritten notes of a class he was taking at East High, beginning February 8, 1915, and ending May 26, 1915. The handwriting is very fluid and attractive, while the spelling and grammar is excellent. There are also several charts he had drawn, and the overall impression of the notebook is that Becker was a serious, hard-working student who took great pride in his class work.

Outside the main entrance to East High, a solitary plaque hangs by the flag pole, in front of the large, concrete stairway, with the following words:

"In memoriam to the boys of this school who gave their lives for freedom's cause. Lieut. Fred H. Becker, '14, died July 18, 1918, at Chateau-Thierry. Pvt. Lynn E. Miller, died October 9, 1916, at Camp Dodge. – In appreciation, East High, Class of 1920."

The memory of Iowa's first All-American athlete had faded considerably through the decades since 1920. Soon after his death, there was talk of naming the Hawkeye football field after Becker and the idea even made it to the floor of the state legislature.

An article with the headline, "A Well Deserved Honor" appeared in a Waterloo newspaper at the time:

"The wonderfully hearty response is being accorded to the suggestion of former Speaker 'Bill' Atkinson that the name of the athletic field at the State University be changed from 'Iowa Field' to 'Becker Field.' It is most gratifying to every man, woman and child in Waterloo.

"Fred Becker was not only a Waterloo boy, he was more – he was a real Iowa boy. He was not only a typical son of our great state in the realm of physical prowess, where he excelled, but he was everything that a young man should be, morally and mentally, as well. He stood for everything that was wholesome, square, honorable, manly and American. He not only stood for them; he did more – he embodied them."

For reasons now forgotten, no action was ever taken. The football stadium at the University of Iowa would not be named after any single individual until the day in 1972 when Iowa's other great athletic hero, also lost during war time, was so honored.

But after publication of a long story about him in the Iowa-Purdue football program in 2008, Fred Becker's name began to fly high again. On September 5, 2009, he was inducted into the University of Iowa Athletics Hall of Fame sponsored by the National Iowa Varsity Club.

"Becker's name had been on the list for several years but I don't think enough was known about him until that article came out in the football program," said Les Steenlage, executive director of the organization. "Once people began to be aware of his amazing story, it didn't take long for him to be voted in."

Among the former Hawkeyes who had been pressing for this honor were Jim Young, a Waterloo native and Hawkeye three-year track letterman, and Bill Windauer, who starred for the Hawkeye football team in the 1970s and played seven years in the NFL.

"I think this award is long overdue," said Young. "I've been working on this for at least three years so it's wonderful that it has finally been accomplished and Fred Becker has been honored in this fashion."

"I am very happy that Fred Becker has been given this recognition," said Windauer. "The youth of America is its oldest tradition. The greatness of our country has been built with their youthful strength, creative minds and strong convictions, from men like Fred Becker, Nile Kinnick, Dan Gable and on and on and on."

Steenlage, an associate athletic director at the University of Iowa, initiated a months-long search to find any living relatives of Fred Becker, but it proved fruitless. Fred had two older sisters, Hilda and Anna, but no trace of their families could be found. Anna married and remained in Waterloo, while Hilda moved to Reading, Pennsylvania, with her husband. At the request of Steenlage, Mike Chapman, a longtime writer and historian who had written the article for the Iowa football program that brought Becker's name back into prominence, represented Becker at the induction.

"It was one of the highlights of my life to stand on the football field named for Nile Kinnick and see Fred Becker honored in such fashion," said Chapman. "It was a moment I will never forget. I would like to imagine that Fred and Nile were together, watching from somewhere."

On February 16, 2010, Becker was inducted into the East High School Athletic Hall of Fame, along with five other athletes. "The Fred Becker story is amazing," said Brenton Shavers, athletic director at the school, in a ceremony prior to the inductions. "It is sad that it was so long forgotten but we are very excited to finally honor Fred Becker here tonight. His story is heroic and inspirational."

With his football accomplishments and his wartime patriotism, Fred Becker stands next to Nile Kinnick as one of Iowa's finest products. One legendary Hawkeye gave his life in World War I while the other perished in World War II. The loss of such leadership potential as both men offered to their state and nation stands as mute testimony to the horrific price of war, for any country. The Fred Becker story needs to be told and re-told as a reminder of the price of freedom, and as an inspiration to young people.

Fred Becker's memory has been resurrected in much the same manner as that of a great athlete named Jack Trice, who lost his life as the result of a startling accident during a football game just five years after Becker died in France.

Jack Trice:

"Two Games, Enduring Fame"

"My thoughts just before the first real college game of my life: The honor of my race, family & self is at stake. Everyone is expecting me to do big things. I will. My whole body and soul are to be thrown recklessly about the field tomorrow."

– Jack Trice, October 5, 1923

Jack Trice:

A Cyclone Legend

He played just one full college football game for Iowa State University and part of another, way back in 1923. Yet, Jack Trice's legacy looms larger than life; in fact, it is of such magnitude that in 1997 ISU named its football stadium in his honor. Though the school has produced numerous first-team All-American football players – including offensive stars such as Dwight Nichols, Dave Hoppmann and George Amundson and defensive standout Matt Blair – the Cyclones now play their home games at Jack Trice Stadium.

But who was Jack Trice? Even though an estimated 300,000 fans every fall stream into a stadium that is named in his honor, very few Iowans know anything about him.

Jack Trice was born in 1902 in Hiram, Ohio, but the exact date is unknown. He was the son of Anna and Green Trice, both of whom were born to slaves.

Green Trice was a free black man who fought for the Union's Tenth Cavalry, an all-black unit, during the Civil War. After the war, he shot buffalo for a living. The occupation sprang into existence as settlers pushed west and the government began building army posts across the Great Plains. At the same time, railroads started their push west and construction crews dotted the landscape, building tracks. Both groups of men, soldiers and construction workers, needed plenty of meat to sustain their hardy existence, and buffalo was the most available and the cheapest. Buffalo hunting became a solid enterprise for the men who were rugged enough to handle the work.

It is estimated that nearly 60 million buffalo were in the Great Plains in the 1860s, when the Indian tribes were the only hunters pursuing the large beasts. But by the 1870s, there were an estimated five thousand buffalo hunters, among them such legendary Old West figures as Wild Bill Hickock, Wyatt Earp and, of course, Buffalo Bill Cody.

By 1884, the great herds were decimated, with an estimated two thousand scattered beasts remaining, a staggering reduction from the vast numbers of just twenty years earlier. Green Trice, Jack's father, returned to Ohio, and enrolled in a school even though he was in his twenties. He was popular with the much younger students for his gentle nature, and for swinging them around at arm's length on the playground.

He also began working on a farm, and met the woman who was to become his wife. He and Anna had just one child, a son they named John, and called Jack. Though there were few other black families in the area, the Trices were readily accepted into the rural community for their work ethic and quiet nature.

When the owner of the farm he was working on died, Green bought the property and looked ahead to a long and prosperous life. But he died unexpectedly from a heart attack in 1909, and Anna was left to raise young Jack by herself. She sold the farm and moved into Hiram, finding work in a laundry and doing sewing at home. Years later, young men who grew up with Jack remembered his mother as a very loving but strict woman. She demanded the best from Jack at all times, in all his ventures.

"When she called, Jack listened, we all did," said one childhood friend. "She was respected by all of us and everyone who knew her." *(14)*

In 1918, with the world war raging overseas and former Hawkeye star Fred Becker serving with the U.S. Marines in France, Anna decided to send her 16 year-old son to Cleveland to live with his aunt and uncle. Anna felt Jack needed to be exposed to a broader range of experiences than were available in the small town of Hiram; in particular, she felt he should be around more members of his own race, as Hiram had a very small black population.

While growing up in Cleveland, Trice exhibited strong athletic skills and a toughness that was undoubtedly inherited from both his father and mother from their own hard lives. He was a standout on the team at East Technical High School, playing for coach Sam Willaman.

A star running back at Ohio State in the 1911 and 1913 seasons, Willaman played pro football for several years. In 1917, he was a member of the famed Canton Bulldogs, playing behind the great Jim Thorpe at halfback and starting some games at the end position. The Bulldogs went 9-1 that season and were declared champions of the pro game.

Willaman developed East Tech into a state power. The team went 7-1 in 1919 with Trice anchoring the line as a sophomore. The next season, the team started 8-0 and outscored the opposition by an amazing 441-0! It won two more games and then was invited to play in Everett, Washington, in what was called a national high school championship.

After a long and tiring train trip of three days duration, Tech lost to the Everett team in front of 20,000 fans, 16-7. Willaman singled out three Tech players for their great play, including Jack Trice.

Jack's final season in high school was just as successful as the first two. The team closed out with an 8-0 record, which included an 89-0 rout over one foe. Trice was named to the all-state football team and the high school yearbook said he was the best tackle to ever play for East Tech.

Willaman's last three seasons had seen Tech post a record of 25-2, and several colleges were interested in luring him away. When the coach was offered the head job at Iowa State College in Ames, he took six of his high school players, including Trice, with him.

But first Willaman had to talk Trice into going to college. After graduation from East Tech, Trice had begun working on a road construction crew. He had also met a young lady named Cora Mae Starland, from nearby Ravenna. Though just fifteen, Cora Mae had fallen in love with the big, handsome football star. She was too young to marry in Ohio without her parent's consent, so they eloped into Monroe, Michigan, to tie the knot. After Willaman convinced Trice into giving college a try, Cora Mae returned to her family's home and Jack went off to Ames alone.

Prior to hiring Willaman, Iowa State had gone through three different coaches in the previous three years. Willaman found measured success and had winning records in three of his four years as head coach. But despite some fine moments turned in by his squads, it seems certain that he would never be able to forget the Minnesota game of October 6, 1923.

Trice spent much of his first year on the Ames campus adjusting to college life. Athletic scholarships were unknown in the 1920s and Trice had very little money so he needed to find a job to help defray costs. He worked as a custodian in the building where he lived off campus, and also for the school's athletic department.

Freshmen were not eligible to compete in football games, so Trice had to be content with scrimmaging against the varsity. Freshmen could participate on the varsity track team, however, and Trice did very well. Big and strong, he won the Missouri Valley Conference freshman championships for Iowa State in the shot put and was fourth in the discus.

Trice was known for his shy manner and his quick smile. Charlie Mayser the school's athletic director, took a liking to him and gave him a key to the school gym. Trice needed the key because he worked there, but the key also allowed him the freedom to come and go into the gym for working out and a sense of pride of being on his own.

"The athletic department job was an important part of Trice's freshman year," wrote Steven L. Jones in the book, *Football's Fallen Hero*. "It allowed the shy college student to make new friends. The job eased the pain of living far from loved ones.

"Because Trice was quiet, few students knew him well. The ones who did saw a friendly person with a warm smile, He always greeted people with a big 'hello.'" *(15)*

Jack couldn't wait for the school year to end so he could get back to Ohio and his young bride. He stayed part of the summer in Ames to work, then took the train home to bring his wife to Iowa. They were startled upon their arrival in Ames on August 6, 1923, to find several thousand persons at the depot; the crowd had gathered to see the funeral train of President Warren G. Harding on its way from San Francisco back east to Washington D.C. Harding just 57, had died of a heart attack on August 2 while on a national speaking tour.

Starting his sophomore year, Jack was one of just twenty black students on campus and life was not easy for the new couple. They had trouble finding housing until a Masonic group allowed them to stay in a room inside the local temple.

Jack and Cora Mae were looking eagerly toward a bright future. Majoring in animal husbandry, Trice planned to move somewhere in the South after graduating from Iowa State and to use his education to work with African-American farmers. Iowa State already enjoyed a reputation for being a leader in offering blacks opportunity in education. In 1891, George Washington Carver became the first black student at the school and after graduating with a degree in botany, he also earned his master's degree in Ames.

By 1921, Carver had become a national figure and was most likely a strong role model for the young Jack Trice. And just down the road in Iowa City there was another superb role model for Trice, this one an athlete of tremendous impact.

The University of Iowa had broken the color barrier several years earlier when Duke Slater arrived on campus in 1918. Slater was a sensational lineman, and in 1921 became the first black player in state history to be named to the All-American first team in football. He had become a folk hero of sorts for his football exploits, playing without a helmet. Slater was a standout on and off the athletic field, and went on to become a highly-respected judge in the Chicago area.

As his sophomore season loomed on the horizon, Trice had matured into a muscular six-foot, 215-pound lineman, an imposing specimen for that day and age. He was certainly well aware that he was about to become the first African-American athlete to ever play football for the college, and one of the very few in the entire Midwest.

Trice started in the line when Iowa State opened the 1923 season on September 29 by hosting Simpson College. The Iowa State stadium, located on the west edge of campus, held about 5,500 fans, and was a little more than half full for the season opener. After a slow start, the Cyclones prevailed, 14-6. Trice blocked a field goal attempt and caused a fumble and received a glowing report in the student newspaper: "In the line, the big colored boy, Jack Trice, is by far the most outstanding performer and gave evidence of being one of the best tackles in the Missouri Valley this year in last weekend's play against Simpson. Trice is fast, strong and a heady player."

The next week found the Cyclones on the road to play the highly-regarded Minnesota Gophers. The team left by train on Thursday evening, and spent Friday in Minneapolis in preparation for the big game. Trice was not allowed to eat in the dining room of the Curtis Hotel where the Iowa State team was staying, and he wound up staying in his room while his teammates ate. When they found out Jack was not permitted to eat with them, the team was upset and protested, but to no avail.

Apparently concerned that he might not play up to his own expectations if he didn't have the proper frame of mind entering the game, Trice wrote a letter to himself the night before, just prior to the final team meeting. He wrote:

"My thoughts just before the first real college game of my life: The honor of my race, family & self is at stake. Everyone is expecting me to do big things. I will. My whole body and soul are to be thrown recklessly about the field tomorrow. Every time the ball is snapped, I will be trying to do more than my part.

"On all defensive plays I must break though the opponents' line and stop the play in their territory. Beware of mass interference. Fight low, with your eyes open and toward the play. Watch out for crossbacks and reverse end runs. Be on your toes every minute if you expect to make good." He signed it "Jack."

The letter was shoved into his suit pocket and wasn't found until several days later. It shows that the young man from Hiram, Ohio, was thoughtful and determined. It also would become a harbinger of the events to come that fateful day, October 6, 1923.

"My whole body and soul are to be thrown recklessly about the field (and) every time the ball is snapped I will be trying to do more than my part ...."

Minnesota played its games at Northrup Field, which could accommodate 27,000 fans. But just 11,000 were on hand for the contest, about 400 of which had come up from Ames. On just the second play of the game, Trice suffered a broken collarbone. He left the game, but he wasn't about to use the injury as an excuse to remain on the sidelines. He told Coach Willaman he wanted back in the game, and he returned a few plays later. He made it through to halftime, with his team tied at 7-7 against the mighty Gophers.

"Trice was playing a great game," wrote Steven Jones. "He had been part of nearly every defensive play. Minnesota had trouble blocking him. Play after play, Trice powered his way into the Gophers' backfield. On offense, Trice tore open wide holes." *(16)*

In the locker room at halftime, the team doctor, Benjamin Dvorak, inspected the collarbone and gave Trice permission to keep playing. But the fateful moment of his young life was just minutes ahead.

With Minnesota on the offense, Trice was in constant motion all over the field. Midway through the period, he threw himself wildly at two blockers and the Gopher ballcarrier, using what is known as a rollback block in an attempt to bring the blockers down and trip up the runner. In the ensuing melee, Trice wound up on his back and was run over by three Minnesota players.

Pulling himself up from the ground, he staggered to the sidelines, with assistance from his teammates. Dvorak checked him carefully and the coaches looked him over too; it was determined he should go to a hospital, but Trice resisted, insisting he wanted back in the game.

In a 1979 interview for the Cleveland Plain-Dealer newspaper, Johnny Behm, one of his teammates explained the situation in more detail:

"The fullback, going through the hole, stepped on Jack's stomach and maybe his groin. He was badly hurt, but tried to get up and wanted to stay in. We saw he couldn't stand and helped him off the field." *(17)*

Dvorak and Trice left the game and went to a local hospital, where doctors looked the stricken athlete over. They told him he could travel home with the team, which wound up losing a hard-fought 20-17 game. Trice left the hospital in time to catch the train back to Ames, but he had not recovered from the trauma he had suffered during the intense game. He lay on a straw mattress in a Pullman coach. Breathing became difficult for him on the ride back, and he was in considerable pain.

Unbeknownst to him and his coaches, he was suffering from internal bleeding and his lungs were hemorrhaging.

Back in Ames, Trice was admitted to the college hospital Sunday morning, with Cora Mae rushing to his side. The pain continued to increase. By late afternoon, Jack was breathing heavily and in terrible pain. But there was little that could be done. A doctor from Des Moines, a specialist in stomach conditions, was consulted and arrived an hour after midnight. After examining the seriously ill athlete, he said he felt surgery was too risky. In mid afternoon, Monday, October 8, two days after the game, Jack Trice died.

Classes were suspended in the afternoon the next day and an estimated four thousand students, faculty and fans attended services which were held on central campus, near the campanile. The casket was covered in cardinal and gold, Iowa State's colors.

There were questions if the injury was the result of a racial bias, or just an unfortunate moment in an extremely tough, physical contest. When Trice was taken from the game in the third period, obviously badly hurt, the Minnesota crowd reportedly chanted, "We're sorry, Ames."

The *University of Minnesota Alumni Weekly* ran a story on October 11, informing its readers of the tragedy.

"Trice was an all-around athlete and a brilliant student," it reported. "His playing ability on the gridiron and his thorough sportsmanship made him one of the most popular students at Ames. In speaking of Trice, Coach (Bill) Spaulding said:

"'He went down fighting and didn't quit. He was a real football player, a hard hitter, but a clean player and a thorough sportsman. Our boys commented after the game on his clean and hard playing. He was a credit to the game.'"

Harry Schmidt, a teammate of Trice, was interviewed in 1954 for a story about his teammate and the fatal game.

"Absolutely not," he responded when asked by writer Bill Walsh if he thought Minnesota had tried to injure Trice on purpose. "I saw the play and was the one who helped him to his feet." *(18)*

Dr. William Thompson, who had coached Trice during his freshman year and saw the Minnesota game, said that Trice had employed "a dangerous block"

Jack Trice, who came to Iowa State from East Technical High School in Cleveland, Ohio, was the grandson of a freed slave and his father had been a buffalo hunter after the Civil War. Here he stands in his Tech lettersweater and cap outside the school entrance in 1920.

(Photos courtesy of Iowa State University Library, Special Collections Department)

An estimated 4,000 fans, students and faculty met near the campanile on October 9, 1923, to remember Jack Trice at a memorial service. He had died the previous day from injuries suffered in a football game at the University of Minnesota.

An artist's tribute to Jack Trice was dedicated on the East Concourse of Jack Trice Stadium in October of 2009. The tribute above includes a sculpture of Trice and traces his athletic career from high school to Iowa State. The work was done by renowned sculptor Ed Dwight, an African-American from Kansas City.

In the photo above, Jack Trice's name greets fans at the stadium's east entrance to Cyclonc football games each fall.

Jack Trice: *"Two Games, Enduring Fame"*

This statue of Jack Trice sits outside Iowa State's football stadium, just east of the Olsen Building. The fifteen-foot tall bronze sculpture is the work of artist Christopher Bennett. A ceremony commemorating the statue and renaming the stadium in Trice's honor was held **August 30, 1997.** *(Photo by Mike Finn)*

where the goal is to throw your body low in an effort to stop the runner, and to wind up rolling to his hands and knees. But Trice wound up on his back, making his abdomen area vulnerable to three other Gopher players following the action. They ran over him.

The Iowa State coaches and fans were shocked by the sudden and tragic turn of events. The powerful and well-spoken young man with the bright future was gone at age 21, struck down in the very prime of life during a sporting event. It was hard to fathom.

The Ames Chamber of Commerce joined forces with the Cardinal Guild to raise funds to pay for the funeral costs and the moving of the body by train to Hiram, where burial was to take place. Nearly $3,000 was donated, with the leftover funds given to his widow and aged mother.

The next Saturday, the team managed to hang on for a 2-0 win over Missouri in Columbia, and then tied Kansas State in Ames, 7-7, on October 20. The Cyclones closed out the season with a 13-6 win over Grinnell, giving them a 4-3-1 record. For the remainder of the season the team wore black armbands in Jack's honor, and the coaches awarded him a varsity letter, which was sent to his mother.

Ironically, the team posted identical records the next two seasons, and then Willaman moved on to coach at Ohio State, his alma mater. He left Ames with a four-year record of 14-15-3 and the painful memories of Jack Trice's tragic end. He was fired in 1933, and died two years later at age 45.

Anna Trice and Jack's uncle Lee, with whom he had lived in Cleveland, came to Ames but missed the funeral due to a mixup with the train scheduling. After a short stay, they were back on the train with the casket and his young widow, headed for Hiram. Cora Mae never returned to Ames, and remarried a few years later. Although she never graduated from college, she had great respect for education and all three of her children earned college degrees.

In a letter written nearly 65 years after the fateful game, on August 3, 1988, from her home in Ponoma, California, she discussed her feelings in eloquent fashion:

"Jack's passing was a great shock to me. He was my first love and I have my beautiful memories of our short life together. The night that he was leaving for Minnesota with his coach, he came to tell me good bye, we kissed and hugged and he told me he would come back to me as soon as he could."

Recalling her visit to the hospital on the fateful day, she wrote: "When I saw him, I said, 'Hello, darling.' He looked at me but never spoke. I remember hearing the campanile chime three o'clock. That was October 8, and he was gone.

"I still have a picture and medals of his high school days, and a necklace that I have treasured through the years."

Jack's mother never fully recovered from the loss of her only son. On October 25, 1923, Anna wrote a poignant letter to Iowa State President R.A. Pearson, providing some insights into her feelings.

"I am proud to know that I am John Trice's mother and proud of the honors that Ames has given to his memory. If there is anything in the life of John Trice and his career at Ames that will be an inspiration to the colored students who will come to Ames, he has not lived his life in vain. But, Mr. President, while I am proud of his honors, he was all that I had and I am old and alone, the future is dreary and lonesome." *(19)*

In 1956, Dr. Gaylord Bates, a boyhood friend of Jack Trice, wrote a letter to the Hiram Township Historical Society, offering his recollections of the Trice family members that he had known decades earlier.

"His mother had a wisdom and dignity admired by all of the women of the community, which must have made itself felt on the boy. She had more tragedies to cope with than anyone should be called upon to bear, being widowed early and losing her only child at the time he offered such great promise." *(20)*

That Jack Trice was a man of tremendous potential seems no doubt. Tributes sprouted up in sports pages across the nation, and several Iowa State college officials wrote stirring letters to honor his work ethic and athletic ability.

Dr. Thompson, the freshman coach in 1922, said "Jack was an outstanding man in any company …. he was a leader in the way that he put out and a leader in desire, I don't believe any boy had more desire than Jack did."

Regarding his football abilities, Thompson added "when the freshmen played the varsity, we had to have two or three men on him ...."*(21)*

Harry Schmidt was another who admired Trice on and off the field "He was a good student and an outstanding athlete, and he would have been All-American (on) all of the teams that could recognize a colored boy at that time." *(22)*

His Cyclone teammates on the 1923 team weren't about to forget Trice and created a plaque that honored his service to Iowa State athletics, repeating the letter he had written to himself the night before the fatal game. The plaque was placed on a wall in the Old Amory. But with time, memories of Trice faded and the plaque became neglected and crusty.

He wasn't pulled back into the spotlight until decades later when the plaque was discovered and was written about by a student. Slowly, the story of Jack Trice came back into focus and by the early 1970s the Cyclones were winning games in record fashion, in old Clyde Williams Field. Plans for a new football stadium were revealed.

Some time in 1973, an athletic department official named Alan Beals saw the old plaque covered in grime and bird droppings. He cleaned it up enough to read it and become curious about Jack Trice's full story. No one in the athletic department knew anything about Trice, but when Beals told Charles Sohn, a member of the English department, what he had found, Sohn swung into action. He invited members of his class to research Trice and write about him.

The class got heavily involved, and voted to begin a move to name the new stadium after the forgotten hero. But there was a long, winding road ahead for them and for Jack Trice.

The Iowa State student body voted to name the new stadium in his honor.

A committee was formed to push for the naming of the stadium for Trice, and over 3,000 signatures were obtained on a petition. Still, there was opposition at the highest levels. In 1983, the new seven-million dollar facility was called Cyclone Stadium, with the playing field named for Trice.

But the student body, even though it turned over every four or five years, was determined to see him honored in even more grand fashion. It began a drive to raise $20,000 for a statue and in 1987 the 1,000-pound, bronze statue was placed outside the stadium. Seven years later, the entire stadium was renamed for the only Cyclone athlete to ever lose his life in an athletic contest.

Jack Trice Stadium was finally dedicated on August 30, 1997. On that day, President Martin C. Jischke issued the following statement:

"It is clear that Jack Trice, for a large majority of students and others associated with Iowa State University, exemplifies a number of heroic qualities, including determination, courage, enthusiasm and giving one's all to an important cause. He has become a hero, not so much because of what he accomplished, because his life was cut short, but for what he represented."

On October 18, 1923, the *Minnesota Alumni Weekly* tried to capture Trice's impact on the game.

"He was a genuine, a thoroughbred. Not daunted by the immensity of the racial vortex into which he had thrown himself, he saw the injustice of that supremacy and fought to prove its fallacy. He knew that if anything was to be accomplished for the Negro race, it must be done through achievement of individuals. It would take the resounding character of a few to show the worth of a race."

Those words still echo today at Jack Trice Stadium in Ames, Iowa – where today's Cyclone football players carry on the spirited enthusiasm of a man who came to Ames over eight decades ago, and became an icon. Trice's legacy has truly stood the test of time. He is the only African-American athlete to have a Division I college football field named for him, and he is most certainly the only football player to be so honored without even playing a full season. Today, a statue of Jack Trice greets visitors to the football stadium where Iowa State University plays its home games each fall.

Several years ago, Ed Dwight was commissioned to make a sculpture of Trice inside the stadium, on the east concourse. The sculpture is a high relief paneled celebration of Trice's story, located on the outer back wall of the Jack Trice Club on the east concourse. It was completed in October of 2009.

The motif depicts Trice's high school career and his journey to Iowa State with Sam Willaman, who had been Trice's prep coach. A presentation of Trice's academic pursuits precedes a visual recounting of his fatal injuries and the large crowd that attended his funeral on campus. There is also a depiction of the student support that galvanized the drive to name the stadium in his honor.

Dwight was the first African-American to attend Bishop Ward High School in Kansas City, Kansas, graduating in 1951, he felt an affinity with Trice and what he endured.

"As the first African-American at my high school, I was told the things I was going to be able to do and the things that I couldn't do," Dwight said. "I know he faced many of the same issues I did, but he did it a generation before I did. He had to be an extraordinary person."

Dwight entered the Air Force in 1953 before graduating with a degree in aeronautical engineering from Arizona State University. In 1961, he was chosen by President John F. Kennedy to enter training to become the first black astronaut. Despite his artistic gifts, Dwight did not begin sculpting until being commissioned in 1974. Today his works are world famous, and Jack Trice is one of his finest examples.

His impact has extended beyond what Jack Trice could have ever imagined back in 1923 when he sat in that lonely hotel room and wrote a letter to himself. More than 85 years later, in another area of Minneapolis, another former Cyclone legend articulated what Jack Trice meant to him.

Matt Blair, like Trice, came to Iowa State from Ohio, but from Dayton rather than Cleveland. Unlike Trice, Blair played two full seasons and in 1973 was an All-American linebacker for the Cyclones. He was drafted by the Minnesota Vikings of the NFL and was a fixture in their defense for 12 seasons, earning All-Pro honors six consecutive years and playing in two Super Bowls.

"During the time I was at Iowa State, I knew who Jack Trice was but I didn't really know any details," said Blair, who in 2009 was voted The Ultimate Cyclone in a poll taken by the Des Moines Register. "I was very surprised when the stadium was named for him, especially when you realize what it must have been like to be a minority athlete back then ….

"What a great inspiration (the naming of the stadium) is to any athlete – that if you play the game the right way you will be respected for what you gave back."

In recent years, Blair learned more about Trice, and was impressed by his story.

"Knowing all the problems you face in life – and then knowing what he faced in 1923 – I have great respect for him as a man. But in his time, an African-American playing football in college – it's awesome," said Blair of Trice. "I never had the honor of playing in the stadium that bears his name, but Jack Trice is a hero to me." *(23)*

Fred Becker died at age 22, and Jack Trice was just 21 when he passed from the scene in 1923. Some twenty years later, on a warm summer day in 1943, the state would lose its greatest football legend at the age of 24. Tragically, their three lives combined could not match the average life span for an adult male in the year 2010!

Jack Trice's story was neglected for decades, but it came roaring back to life in the 1980s and '90s. Now, it is doubtful that he will ever be forgotten again – not as long as college football is an integral part of American life.

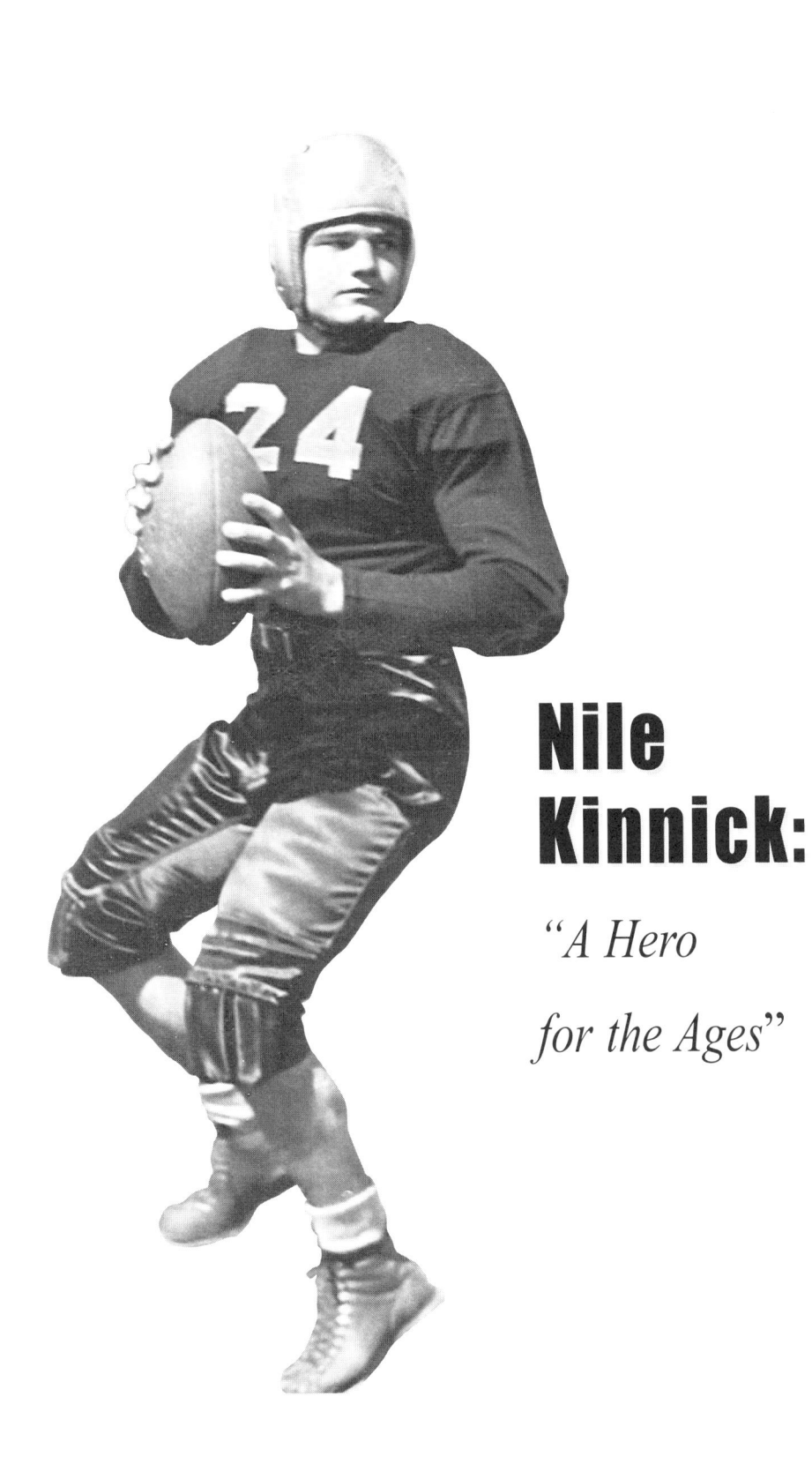

Nile Kinnick:

"A Hero for the Ages"

In 1939, "a coach who doubled as a surgeon, a 5-foot-8 farm boy they called the 'Cornbelt Comet' and a squad of football players who played offense, defense and sometimes the entire game captured the imagination of the college football world."

– Iowa City-Press Citizen. (24)

Nile Kinnick:

The Greatest Hawkeye

At five foot eight inches tall, he would hardly be noticed walking across a college campus, even back in 1939 when Americans were smaller. In today's world, he wouldn't even be considered average size for a 22-year-old male.

Many of those who saw him on the University of Iowa campus in the years between 1937 and 1940 remembered that he was always carrying several books and that he had a quick smile for anyone who looked his way.

Despite the incredible acclaim that came during his final year of college athletics, he appeared totally unaffected. He continued in the same humble style that he had learned from his parents while growing up in Adel, Iowa.

Nile Clarke Kinnick was one of a kind, the best of the best – an incredible athlete, superb scholar and terrific leader. The grandson of a governor, he was raised in a strong and loving family in the heartland of America – and became a Cornbelt Comet shooting across the night sky. And then, at age 24, he was gone. He left behind a legacy that has inspired countless Iowans to strive to reach their fullest potential, and to never accept anything but the very best from oneself.

In 1939, he led a tiny band of college football players into immortality. Known as "The Ironmen," they epitomized the America generation that had fought through the Great Depression and was then left facing World War II. And Nile

Kinnick was the greatest Ironman of them all.

During his short lifetime, Kinnick was a hero on many stages; in death, he became an enduring legend. His list of accomplishments, both on and off the athletic field, was one of a kind:

- Consensus All-American football player in 1939
- Big Ten's Most Valuable Player (the largest vote margin ever)
- Heisman Trophy (the largest margin in history at that time)
- Walter Camp Award as the top college player of the year
- Maxwell Award as the top college player of the year
- Associated Press's top male athlete of 1939 (over Joe Louis, Joe DiMaggio and Byron Nelson)
- President of senior class at University of Iowa
- Phi Beta Kappa scholar
- Delivered the commencement address at 1940 Iowa graduation
- Turned down lucrative offers to play pro football
- Entered law school at Iowa (ranked third in class after first year)
- Left law school to become a navy pilot
- Selected to College Football Hall of Fame (inaugural class of 1951)
- Voted to All-Time College Football Team
- *College Football News* ranked him the 9th greatest college player of all time
- Captain of the All-Time University of Iowa football team
- His image is on the coin flipped at the start of every Big Ten football game
- Iowa's football stadium is named after him (the only Heisman Trophy winner so honored)
- A high school in Japan is named after him
- His jersey number (24) is retired (one of just two at Iowa)
- Still held several Iowa records 50 years after his last game

Truth be told, there's never been an athlete quite like Nile Kinnick in all of college history. And it all started in Adel, today a community of some 3,500 persons situated just 30 miles northwest of Des Moines, in prime Iowa farm country.

The Kinnick clan came to America in the late 1770s from Holland, settling in Maryland. They journeyed west, to Indiana, and finally arrived in Iowa in 1854. Settling in the area of Adel, the Kinnick name became a fixture in local business, farming and politics. Nile's paternal grandfather, Will, was the youngest of three boys. The two oldest brothers left to fight in the Civil War, on behalf of the Union, and when their father died suddenly, Will was left alone at home to farm nearly 400 acres of prime Iowa land.

Will Kinnick married Mary Jane Stump, who lived on a farm in the Des Moines area, and they raised five children – the youngest of whom was Nile Clarke Kinnick, Sr. The name "Nile" came from the Stump side of the family and has a Celtic origin which means, roughly, "courageous warrior." It was a word that would come to have great meaning for the family.

The Kinnick name was notable in the Adel area for decades. Not only was Will Kinnick a successful farm owner and operator and owner of a large home in the city, he was involved in numerous civic ventures. He served on the Adel city council and was a member of the county board of supervisors for two terms. Even today, visitors to the courthouse in the center of Adel can read his name on the plaque inside the main entrance.

Nile Sr. was born on a farm three miles north of Adel; five years later, the family (without his mother, Mary Jane, who died two years after Nile Sr. was born) moved into a house in Adel, at 219 North 12th Street. Built in 1900, the two-story wood framed structure would be home to the Kinnick family until 1934. All three of Nile Sr.'s boys were born and raised in the home, still standing at 219 North 12th Street.

He graduated from Iowa State University in 1916 with a degree in agronomy. While at Iowa State, he played three years of collegiate football, though weighing just one hundred and thirty five pounds. He was a quarterback and was adept at drop-kicking, a trait that would be keenly developed by his son during his football days at the other college down the road, in Iowa City, two decades later.

Nile Sr. and Frances Clarke met during their school days and quickly became a steady pair. They finished one-two in the Adel High School class rankings (she was first, he was second), graduating in the spring of 1912. While he moved on to Ames, she attended Drake College in Des Moines at first, then transferred to Northwestern in Evanston, Illinois, where she studied voice. It was also in Evanston that she became a Christian Science follower.

Though Frances had her heart set on a career as a professional concert singer, she gave it up to come back to Adel and marry Nile Sr. They moved into the family house on North 12th Street and eventually had three sons – Nile Jr., Ben and George. The boys didn't have far to go to high school. In fact, all they had to do was cross the street. Adel High school was just a football toss away.

When the United States entered World War I on April 6, 1917, Nile Sr. assumed he would be drafted and sent overseas. His number was never called, however, and he stayed busy with the farming chores.

"…. his part in the war was typical of many young men in the granary of the nation – to produce all he could to feed the troops and the hungry of the world," wrote D.W. Stump in his 1975 biography, *Kinnick: The Man and the Legend*. "A deep sense of responsibility, throughout preparation and diligent execution of one's duties (a Kinnick family tradition) was put to work in the service of the nation." *(25)*

Nile Kinnick Jr. was born on July 9, 1918 – just nine days before Fred Becker, Iowa's first All-American, was killed in France. He was the eldest son. Ben followed just thirteen months later, while George appeared on October 19, 1926. It was a rather idyllic childhood for the Kinnick boys, growing up in a loving family environment where everyone was encouraged to work hard and dream big. Life was split between the large house in town and doing chores on the family farms, owned and operated by uncles and cousins.

Nile's youth was one of constant activity and learning. He attended school, handled some farm chores and participated in rough-and-tumble football games in the Kinnick front yard in the fall. In the winter, he played basketball in a barn where his dad had rigged up baskets, and went ice skating on the Raccoon River with family and friends. He played marbles in the spring and baseball in the summer.

He also worked hard to earn spending money. At age nine, he took on a newspaper route for the Des Moines Register; he worked as a bagger at a grocery store at age twelve, and also found time to cut weeds and shovel grain.

All the time, the Kinnick household was filled with conversation after supper, with the parents engaging their children in lively discussions about a wide variety of subjects. In the Kinnick home, thinking was as important as playing.

At Adel Junior High School, Nile was a three-sport star, excelling in football, basketball and baseball. He helped the team to undefeated seasons in both football and basketball. He continued the same success in high school, and in 1933, his junior year, Adel posted its first undefeated season ever in football.

The Des Moines Register, the same paper that Nile used to deliver on Adel doorsteps, reported thusly: "Kinnick, who directed the Adel team from the quarterback position, liked the rough going and he played fiercely in every tilt of a 12-game schedule. Kinnick was versatile …. and carried the ball brilliantly in the open field. His passing and punting figured prominently in every Adel game."

Adel was voted the state mythical title, and today a football signed by every member of the Adel team of 1933 can be seen in a trophy case at Adel-Minborn-Desoto High School.

Nile was involved in far more than athletics at school. Encouraged by his parents and one of his favorite coaches, Otto Kohl, he participated in both speech contests and drama, and worked very hard at his studies. He maintained a near straight-A average all through high school.

When basketball season rolled around, Kinnick proved he was just as skilled on the court as he was on the football field. He scored one-third of the team's point that season as it fought its way to the finals of the district playoffs. He scored 25 points in a losing cause at districts and drew rave reviews from the newspapers. As great as was his junior year in both football and basketball, it looked like his senior year would be one of the finest in the history of Iowa high school athletics.

But it wasn't to be. With the Great Depression in full swing, the economy bottomed out all across the Midwest. The Kinnicks lost much of their wealth and the family farms were, in the words of Nile Sr., "swept away." He accepted a position as a farm appraiser for the Federal Land Bank in Omaha, about seventy miles to the west. Suddenly, young Nile was saying goodbye to Adel, where he had spent all previous seventeen years of his life. He was destined to become a Benson

Bunny!

At Benson High School, he treated Nebraska fans and sportswriters to the same sort of show he had given Adel. He was a sensation on the football field, several times hooking up with brother Ben for scoring strikes. In a 27-0 victory over Fremont, he ran wild on the field and he scored numerous other times during the season on dazzling runs. At the end of the season he was named first team all-state.

That winter, he led the basketball team to third place in the state tournament and wound up being named first team all-state in that sport, as well.

A player from the Abraham Lincoln High School in Council Bluffs didn't hold anything back when talking about his basketball skills: "He was a sight to behold. I had never seen a basketball player of his abilities up 'til that time. His dribbling with either hand and all-around ball handling, ability to change speed and direction were uncanny, to say nothing of his accurate shooting." *(26)*

He also played catcher on the Benson baseball team and helped it win the city championship. He had always done well in baseball, dating all the way back to the time he played American Legion summer baseball, on an area team that also included Bob Feller, of nearby Van Meter. In fact, several times when Feller was pitching, Kinnick was the catcher.

Within a few years, they would be two of the most celebrated athletes in the entire nation, and future hall of famers!

While playing three sports at Benson, Nile was maintaining the straight A grade-point average he had brought with him from Adel. He was also very popular off the field, showing as much attention to the second and third-team players as he did to the starters.

"I am sure that those of us who grew up with Nile were aware we were with an outstanding individual, who let his actions and deeds speak for him," recalled Randy Mortimer, an Adel teammate, years later. "He was humble, almost to the point of being shy, where his abilities were concerned."

Although Kinnick was a gifted natural athlete, those who knew him well understood that he worked extremely hard to hone his skills.

"Nile was the leader, organizer and coach," said Mortimer. "He was always working to improve and perfect his talents and abilities in all sports. Nile took part in other school activities, such as plays and speech contests. He was a leader in the classroom just as he was on the field of sports." *(27)*

He followed in the footsteps of his father when it came to kicking a football. He spent hours working on his kicking techniques, and developed extraordinary control of the trajectory. It was a skill that would play a huge role in Iowa's incredible triumph over Notre Dame several years later in Iowa City. He also worked on throwing a football so well that he could toss it equally well with either hand, though he was not ambidextrous by nature.

With high school behind him, Nile decided it was time for a big trip out west. He and Ben took off in the family's 1929 Ford Coupe, and spent two weeks on the road. They drove through Colorado, sleeping in farmer's fields a couple of nights, and down into New Mexico, then over to Los Angeles and up the coast to Seattle, visiting relatives.

During the long drive, Nile had plenty of time to contemplate his upcoming college years. Recruiting was nothing at all like it was to become in the decades ahead, and college coaches confined their efforts to a letter or two and maybe a visit in the home, if the prospect was really sensational.

Both Drake University and Iowa State showed interest in the son of one of their graduates, but Nile entertained visions of playing at the University of Minnesota. Under coach Bernie Bierman, the Golden Gophers had won two national titles in the 1930s and were considered, with Notre Dame, one of the top two football schools in the country.

"When Nile was a senior, Bernie Bierman was top dog in the Big Ten, so Nile drove up to Minneapolis to see if the Gophers had any interest in him," said Nile Sr., in an exclusive 1989 interview with Maury White of the Des Moines Register. "They didn't, not at all. Not many people know that. So he came back to Iowa….

"Otto Kohl, who had been his coach at Adel, took Nile to Iowa City and introduced him to Rollie Williams, the basketball coach whom he knew well, and to Ossie Solem, the football coach. They offered him a job and he worked a few weeks there that summer, digging ditches. Nile chose Iowa because of the law school." *(28)*

Bierman's decision would come back to haunt him in a stunning fashion four years later. Looking back with the perspective of time, it simply seems that Nile Kinnick was destined to become a Hawkeye – and destined to become the greatest football player in Iowa history!

Nile Kinnick enrolled at Iowa in the fall of 1936, and attracted attention almost immediately. Elected co-captain of the freshman team, Kinnick ran 25 yards for one touchdown and passed 24 yards for another in a scrimmage against the varsity. A Chicago writer predicted he would become one of the Big Ten's brightest stars.

In order to excel in college sports, Kinnick had to overcome his relatively small stature. But he was very muscular and had a terrific athletic aptitude. He had great natural skills, worked extremely hard and was a perfectionist, spending hours on drills for passing and kicking.

Erwin Prasse, who was to become Kinnick's favorite passing target, came to Iowa City from a Chicago high school and recalled his first impression of Kinnick.

"When I got there and suited up, I thought I had gone to the wrong place because everyone was so big," Prasse said decades later. "Then I saw Kinnick and I thought, 'If this little guy can stick it out, so can I.'"

At the end of Kinnick's freshman year, Ossie Solem was fired and Irl Tubbs became the new football coach. Iowa was just 1-7 in Kinnick's sophomore year, 1937, but the former Adel prep star showed great promise. His brightest moment came against Michigan, when he returned a punt 74 yards for a touchdown, in a 7-6 loss. He also led the nation in punting with an average of 43 yards a kick.

He was voted first team All-Big Ten by United Press, which wrote he was "Iowa's dynamic sophomore who stared defeat in the eye every Saturday without batting an eye." He was also selected to the third team of the All-American squad announced by Newspaper Enterprise Association.

Kinnick played basketball his freshman and sophomore years at Iowa, becoming a starter on the varsity his second season. He scored 75 points during the season and helped the team with his skilled ball handling. He was the leading scorer in several games, but at season's end he gave up the sport in order to concentrate on his studies.

"I like basketball very much but I came here primarily to get an education and rather than let the sport interfere with my school work, I've decided to drop it," he said.

"Naturally, I hate to lose him but Nile knows his own mind," said Coach Rollie Williams. "He's serious about his studies and if he's afraid that basketball will interfere with his scholastic ambitions, then it's probably the best that he does not turn out."

For the 1938 football season, Iowa went 1-6-1. Bothered by a sore ankle, Nile missed a good portion of the season and slipped to honorable mention All-Big Ten. Both the team and its future star were left to ponder what was transpiring and the future didn't look very bright.

And then came 1939.

After just two years at the helm, Tubbs was replaced as head coach by Eddie Anderson, a former star player at Notre Dame. A native of Oskaloosa, Iowa, Anderson had played high school football at Mason City. At Notre Dame, he had rubbed shoulders with the immortals of Fighting Irish football – Knute Rockne had been his coach and George Gipp ("win one for The Gipper") was a teammate.

As a coach, Anderson earned a national reputation at Holy Cross College, going 47-7-4 in six seasons. He had earned a degree in medicine and was Dr. Eddie Anderson by the time he arrived in Iowa City to try and make Iowa a football power once again. He was a fanatic about conditioning and his practice sessions at Iowa were so tough that of the 80 men who showed up for tryouts on the first day, only 35 were still around when the season began.

At Iowa, he and Nile became friends immediately. While Anderson called every other player by his last name, he always referred to Nile by his first name. They also became heroes the likes of which the state had never seen before on an athletic field. Because most of the small squad played the entire 60 minutes of every game, they eventually became know as "Ironmen."

Kinnick was very excited about the new attitude in camp prior to the start of the season. He had worked extremely hard to get in top shape for his final campaign.

Brimming with confidence, he wrote to his parents about his new enthusiasm: "For three years – nay, for fifteen years – I have been preparing for this last year of football. I anticipate becoming the roughest, toughest back to yet hit this conference."

It was uncharacteristic for Kinnick to be so bold, but the letter underscores the determination that was driving him to excel in his final season. It was destined to be a performance that no Hawkeye fan would ever forget.

In the opener against South Dakota, Kinnick scored three touchdowns, tossed a 63-yard scoring strike to Russell Buck and kicked five extra points in the 41-0 win. Only 16,000 fans saw the game in Iowa City.

The second game was a terrific, come-from-behind 32-29 win over Indiana, with Kinnick throwing a dramatic touchdown (his third of the game) to Erwin Prasse with just two minutes left in the game. He set an Iowa record by returning nine punts for 201 yards, a record that stood for over 50 years. He rushed for 103 yards on 19 carries and completed four passes for 103 yards. He added another 171 yards on six kickoff returns and 20 more on an interception of a Hoosier pass. All total, Kinnick accounted for 603 yards on the day. It was an amazing performance!

In the third game at Michigan, the Wolverines dealt Iowa a 27-7 loss. Running back Tom Harmon (who was to finish second behind Nile in the Heisman balloting) had four touchdowns and quarterback Forest Evashevski (who would coach Iowa to national prominence 15 years later) was a standout. Kinnick threw one touchdown pass.

Game No. 4 was a 19-13 win for Iowa at Wisconsin, with Kinnick throwing three touchdowns passes, to three different receivers. This time, it was his passing that made the difference. In other games, it was his running and kicking. And always, it was his leadership.

He was one of five men to play all 60 minutes and after the game Coach Anderson referred to his team as "Ironmen" for the first time. It was a nickname destined to become the most famous in Hawkeye sports history.

In the fifth game, Iowa was on the road for the third straight week, and defeated a rugged Purdue team 4-0 on two safeties. Nile was one of eight Hawkeyes who played the entire game, on both offense and defense, and his booming punts kept the Boilermakers off balance the entire game. He finished with 65 yards rushing against the bruising Purdue defense, by far the best total of any back on either team.

Returning home, unbeaten and top-rated Notre Dame was Iowa's sixth foe. Kinnick was superb, punting the ball 16 times for an average of 46 yards and keeping the Fighting Irish pinned deep in their own territory nearly the entire game. His last punt of 67 yards bounced out of bounds on the Notre Dame five-yard line and put the game out of reach.

On offense, he switched positions from left to right halfback in the closing minutes of the second period and bolted through the line for a dramatic touchdown. The photo has become one of the most famous in Hawkeye history. He also kicked the extra point as Iowa pulled off a stunning upset, 7-6. His teammates carried Nile off the field on their shoulders. Classrooms were nearly empty on Monday as the celebration continued and the Hawkeyes were mobbed just about anywhere they went the entire week.

The victory drew considerable national attention and set the stage for one of the greatest showdowns in Hawkeye history. For the seventh game, 50,000 fans jammed into the Iowa stadium for the game with powerful Minnesota.

The Gophers led 9-0 entering the final period, and then Kinnick went to work. He threw a long touchdown pass to Prasse and kicked the extra point, to make it 9-7, Minnesota. In the closing minutes, Kinnick took his team down field again and threw a perfect strike to Bill Green, deep in the end zone. The Hawkeyes won, 13-9; the upstart team was suddenly 6-1 on the season and the toast of the entire nation.

Sportswriter James S. Kearns of the Chicago Daily News was so impressed that he could hardly contain himself:

"There's a golden helmet riding on a human sea across Iowa's football field in the twilight here. Now the helmet rises as wave upon wave of humanity pours onto the field. There's a boy under the golden helmet which is shining like a crown on his head. A golden No. 24 gleams on his slumping, tired shoulders.

"The boy is Nile Clarke Kinnick, Jr., who has just now risen above all the defenses that could be raised against him. He has gone out of Iowa's domestic football scene with an explosive, dramatic, incredible farewell party of his own making. He has just thrown the great power and size of Minnesota into a 13-9 defeat before an overflow crowd of 50,000.

"Here was courage incarnate, poise personified in the calm deliberation of a 21-year-old boy. Here was Kinnick at the peak of his great career, leading a frenzied little band of football players to a victory which was impossible. They couldn't win, but they did."

Here's how another Chicago writer told the story: "Nile Kinnick 13, Minnesota 9; tersely, that tells the story of the most spectacular football game in modern Big Ten history."

Among those in the stands that day was a young graduate named Paul Morrison, who was about to embark upon an amazing career as sports information director at Drake University. At Drake, Morrison was destined to see every single game Johnny Bright played.

"I've never seen a game like that one," said Morrison in 2010, some 92 years of age and an icon in the Drake athletic offices. "It was the greatest game I ever saw. I can still see the Iowa players carrying Kinnick off the field on their shoulders."

The Ironmen's final game, on the field of nationally-ranked Northwestern University, was an anti-climax. Kinnick had played seven full games without one moment on the sidelines, but he severely injured his right shoulder in the early going and was forced to sit out the rest of the game on the bench. With their star on the sidelines, the Hawks were ineffective in moving the football and had to settle for a 7-7 tie with the Wildcats.

It was an amazing season for a school that hadn't seen a winning team for nearly a decade. The Hawkeyes closed out at 6-1-1 and were ranked ninth in the nation by the Associated Press.

The season probably wasn't a real shock to at least one former Adel high school player who had been a Kinnick teammate. Randy Mortimer had grown accustomed to seeing the fabulous athlete do similar feats in other games many years earlier.

"One always had the feeling, when the going was the toughest and the outlook the darkest, that Nile would figure a way to pull the game out of the fire," said Mortimer decades later. *(29)*

At season's end, the honors showered over Kinnick. He was everybody's first team All-American halfback, and was named the Big Ten's Most Valuable Player by the largest margin ever. He outdistanced Michigan's talented Harmon for the Heisman Trophy by a 651-405 margin. Nile and Eddie Anderson were flown to New York City to participate in the awarding of the Heisman Trophy by the New York Downtown Athletic Club.

Taking center stage and looking resplendent in a pin-striped suit, Kinnick held the audience spellbound with what is still considered the finest acceptance speech in Heisman history.

"Thank you very, very kindly, Mr. Holcomb," he began, addressing the master of ceremonies. "It seems to me that everyone is letting their superlatives run away with them this evening. Nonetheless, I want you to know that I'm mighty, mighty happy to accept this trophy this evening.

"Every football player in these United States dreams about winning that trophy, and of this fine trip to New York. Every player considers that trophy to be the acme in recognition of this kind. And the fact that I am actually receiving this trophy tonight almost overwhelms me, and I know that all those boys who have gone before me must have felt somewhat the same way.

"From my own personal viewpoint, I consider my winning this award as, indirectly, a great tribute to the new coaching staff at the University of Iowa, headed by Dr. Eddie Anderson, and to my teammates sitting back in Iowa City. A finer man and a better coach never hit these United States, and a finer bunch of boys and more courageous bunch of boys never graced the gridirons of the Midwest than that Iowa team of 1939. I wish that they might all be with me tonight to receive this trophy. They certainly deserve it.

"I want to take this grand opportunity to thank, collectively, all the sportswriters and all the sportscasters and all those who have seen fit, have seen their way clear to cast a ballot in my favor for this trophy. And I also want to take this opportunity to thank Mr. Prince, his committee, the Heisman Award Committee, and all those connected with the Downtown Athletic Club for this trophy, and for the fine time that they're showing me …. and not only for that, but for making this fine and worthy trophy available to the football players of this country.

"Finally, if you will permit me, I'd like to make a comment which in my mind is indicative, perhaps, of the greater significance of football and sports emphasis in general in this country, and that is I thank God I was warring on the gridirons of the Midwest and not the battlefields of Europe. I can speak confidently and positively that the players of this country would much more, much rather, struggle and fight to win the Heisman award than the Croix de Guerre. Thank you."

As Kinnick walked back to his seat, the New York crowd erupted in a standing ovation. And the superlatives continued to flow.

"…. the ovation wasn't alone for Nile Kinnick, the outstanding college football player of the year," wrote Whitney Martin of the Associated Press. "It was also for Nile Kinnick, typifying everything admirable in American youth."

Bill Cunningham of the Boston Globe said it even better: "This country's okay as long as it produces Nile Kinnicks. The football part is incidental."

Knowing Kinnick's passion for history, it is reasonable to conclude that he might have made mention of the Croix de Guerre because of the fact that Fred Becker had been awarded the honor some twenty-one years earlier. Jim Young, a three-year Hawkeye letterwinner in track in the 1950s, has studied the careers of both Becker and Kinnick and retired after a long career as a college history professor. Young thinks it is a reasonable assumption that Kinnick did know that Becker had been given the award.

There were many more honors ahead for Kinnick. He was selected college football's finest player by two other organizations, those that gave out the Maxwell Award and the Walter Camp Award. Incredibly, he was named the Associated Press Male Athlete of the Year, with Joe DiMaggio of the New York Yankees and Joe Louis, world heavyweight boxing champion, finishing second and third, respectively.

Other members of the Iowa team were also honored for their efforts that

Frances Kinnick relaxes with her sons Nile (right), Ben (left), and George (on her lap) at the Kinnick family home in Adel. Their father, Nile Sr., is seen in the inset photo.

One of the finest kickers in the history of college football, Nile led the nation in punting in 1937 and his incredible kicking against Notre Dame in 1939 was the key to Iowa's stunning victory. Here he practices his punting under the watchful eye of assistant coach Frank Carideo, an All-America star at Notre Dame a few years earlier.

In one of the most famous photos in Hawkeye football history, Nile Kinnick crashes the line to score the only touchdown in Iowa's 7-6 upset of mighty Notre Dame in Iowa City. Kinnick, battered and bruised, was carried off the field by his teammates after the game.

To this day, Nile Kinnick is considered the ideal student athlete. Not only was he an All-America football player and basketball starter, he was a Phi Beta Kappa scholar and president of the senior class of the University of Iowa.

An all-state basketball player in high school at both Adel and in Omaha, Kinnick was a starter on the Hawkeye basketball team his sophomore year but passed up his final two seasons to concentrate on his studies and on football.

(This photo and Hawkeye football photos courtesy of the University of Iowa Athletic Department.)

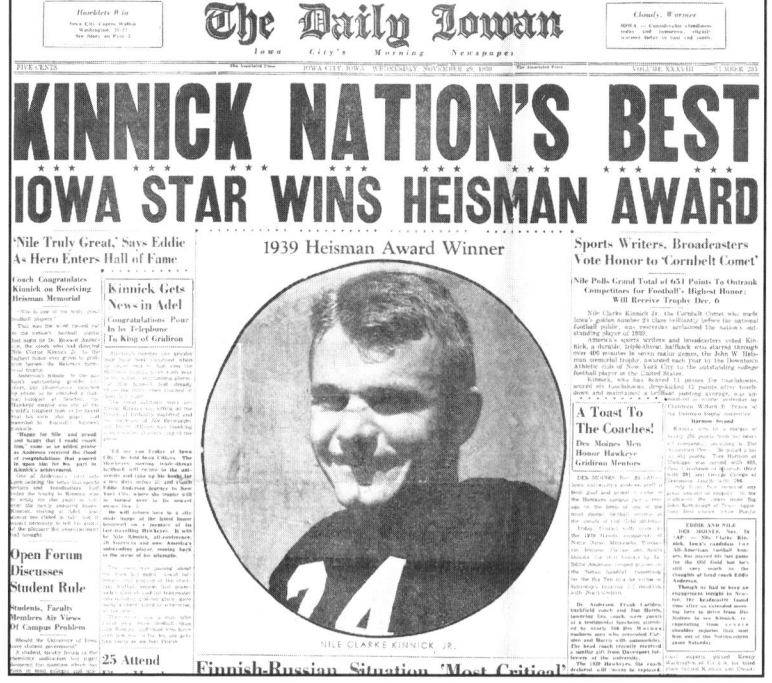

This headline in the University of Iowa student newspaper announces that Iowa's legendary football star has just won the 1939 Heisman Trophy.

Shortly after receiving the Heisman Trophy in New York City, Nile Kinnick poses for the camera with his award. His acceptance speech is widely considered the finest Heisman Trophy speech ever given.

In 1940, Kinnick was the leading vote getter in the prestigious College All-Star football game held each summer at Soldier Field in Chicago. The game pitted top college seniors against the NFL champions. In the photo above, Kinnick (carrying ball) runs a practice with the All-Star backfield; in the photo below, he runs for yardage during the game. Nile threw for two touchdowns and kicked four extra points in the last football game he ever played.

Nile Kinnick: *"A Hero for the Ages"*

After his incredible senior season, Nile Kinnick was in demand for speeches and public appearances all over the state and he was happy to oblige. In the larger photo, he is mobbed by young fans as he signs an Iowa pennant and in the smaller photo he visits a young man in a local hospital.

In December of 1942, Ensign Nile Kinnick was assigned to the aircraft carrier U.S.S. Lexington, one of 24 Essex-class carriers built during World War II. It was large enough to hold 5,000 men, and could have supported three football fields or one thousand cars on its main deck. It would be his last home. Today (above), it is a museum on the bay in Corpus Christi, Texas. *(Photo by Mike Chapman)*

Ensign Nile Kinnick flew off the deck of this ship (at the marker number 16) in the Gulf of Paria on June 2, 1943, and never returned. *(Photo courtesy of U.S.S. Lexington)*

On December 4, 1941, three days before the Empire of Japan bombed Pearl Harbor, Nile Kinnick was called to active duty with the Naval Reserve Air Corps. It was the pivotal moment in his young life. He had his photo taken (left) after getting his officer's commission and later as a pilot standing next to his plane on the deck of the U.S.S. Lexington.

season. Prasse was named first team All-Big Ten at end and second team All-American, while Mike Enich, a powerful lineman, was also all conference and a third team All-American. In addition, Iowa finished ninth in the final AP poll, and Eddie Anderson was selected coach of the year.

Many years later, Anderson wrote about Iowa's incredible victory over Minnesota in glowing terms. "I've had many great days as a player and coach …. but I doubt if I'll ever experience again the glory of the day that Nile Kinnick gave me in 1939. They named me coach of the year in 1939, but there is no doubt that the glory belonged to Iowa and Kinnick, the best football player of 1939 and one of the greatest and most courageous I have ever seen." *(30)*

While Kinnick was honing his athletic skills at Iowa, he was hardly neglecting his studies. He had entered Iowa with an A average out of high school and kept his grades at a 3.4 level in college. He graduated in the top five percent of his class in 1940, and was admitted to the Phi Beta Kappa honorary fraternity. He was also voted president of the Iowa senior class and then, at a meeting of Big Ten class presidents in Chicago, was voted president of that group.

In addition, he was the top vote getter in the prestigious College All-Star Football Game, which was held each summer at Soldier Field in Chicago. The game pitted the top college football players against the champions of the National Football League. Held on August 29, 1940, it was the last football game Nile Kinnick would ever participate in. He threw for two touchdowns and kicked four extra points in a 45-28 loss to the Green Bay Packers.

Professional football was growing in popularity in the late 1930s, and Kinnick was a first round draft choice of the Philadelphia Eagles of the National Football League. He was also offered a very comfortable contract of $10,000 a year or $1,000 a game, a large amount of money for the era, from the Brooklyn Dodgers football team. One of the team owners, Dan Topping, even flew to Iowa City with his wife, Sonja Henie, a movie actress and former Olympic figure skating champion, and took Nile out to dinner in an effort to sign him. But it was to no avail.

Kinnick turned his back on pro football to enter law school at Iowa. In his first year, despite helping coach the freshman football team, he ranked third in a class of 104 law students.

Politics was now prominently on his mind. His maternal grandfather, George W. Clarke, had served as governor of Iowa for two terms, from 1913 to 1917, and was an inspiration to his grandson. At the request of the Young Republican Party, Kinnick joined Governor George Wilson and presidential candidate Wendell Wilkie at several locations on the campaign trail. He introduced the pair to a huge crowd in Iowa Falls and drew resounding cheers when he took to the podium. Wilkie was so impressed that he reportedly said Kinnick should be running for president instead of him!

A dynamic speaker with a quick smile and pleasing personality, Kinnick seemed tailor-made for a career in politics. But it was not to be. In August of 1941, Kinnick had determined that war was imminent and he joined the Naval Air Corps Reserve. It would turn out to be the most monumental decision of his entire life. On December 4, he reported for duty on a base at Fairfax Airport northeast of Kansas City.

The Japanese bombing of Pearl Harbor on December 7, 1941, changed the world forever. It propelled the United States full force into World War II, with millions of men and women going into harm's way. Among those who would pay the ultimate price for America's involvement was the most decorated athlete in Iowa history.

Kinnick was in officer's training when word of the Pearl Harbor disaster struck. He was sent briefly to a base in New Orleans on February 3, 1942, and then to bases in Jacksonville and Pensacola, Florida. He received his officer's commission in Miami and was sent to Norfolk, Virginia, for more pilot training. Then he was assigned to fighter pilot group 16 and learned he would be sent eventually to an aircraft carrier.

After basic training, he began keeping a diary, exposing some of his innermost feelings. The details of the diary were printed in a remarkable book, *A Hero Perished*, published by the University of Iowa Press in 1991. Clearly, at that point sports had disappeared almost entirely from his sphere of importance. As a youth and young man, athletics had been a proving ground, a means to test himself, but after graduation from Iowa in the spring of 1940 he moved far beyond the narrow confines of an athletic field. He had spurned offers to play professionally for a reason: Nile Kinnick was now marching to a different drummer.

The young Hawkeye star was not at all interested in living in his past glories but was always looking forward to new horizons. He expressed some doubts about the perils that lay ahead but, in typical Kinnick fashion, he was resolute in his determination to face anything in his path.

"Every man whom I have admired in history has willingly and courageously served his country's armed forces in time of danger," he wrote to his parents. "It is not only a duty, but an honor to follow their examples as best I can.

"I hope God will give me the courage and the ability to conduct myself in every situation that my country, my family and my friends will be proud of me."

With no college courses to keep his always-active mind busy, Kinnick often found himself bored. He did a considerable amount of reading during this period of his life, including such fine works of literature as *Grapes of Wrath* by John Steinbeck and *War and Peace*, the 1,300-page novel by Leo Tolstoy, and other classics. He devoured biographies of Abe Lincoln, Teddy Roosevelt and Winston Churchill, whom he deeply admired. He studied and engaged anyone who came within earshot on a variety of subjects. And always, he was reflecting on the largest issues of life.

"What a magnificent job the Russians are doing," he wrote in his diary, concerning their efforts in the early stages of the war. Then, he added prophetically: "What is to keep them from overrunning all of Europe? What a problem the U.S. will have with Communists …. must England and the U.S. end up fighting that outfit too…. it looks like a pretty rough and rocky road ahead."

He enjoyed movies, and went to them frequently while living on the various service bases, and dined out whenever possible. He wrote continually – in his diary, to his family and to friends. He loved receiving letters, and was disappointed when they didn't come more frequently.

"Don't seem to get much mail anymore …. rather depressing, too, there are several people who owe me letters," he wrote on April 22, 1942.

An ominous note was registered in his diary on July 2, 1942. His fighter pilot group was given instructions in hand-to-hand combat and water survival. Of the later, he wrote: "We had swim test at 11 a.m. Had to stay afloat (could move arms & legs) for five minutes without a rest. Sounds simple, but I found that 5 minutes can be an awfully long time."

Less than a year later, he would ditch his plane in the Gulf of Paria, and be in desperate need of all the water survival skills he had ever learned.

On July 8, he wrote: "My birthday – 24 years on this mortal coil – happy, strenuous, endeavoring years – and what of the future? Can't view it with pessimism despite the circumstances."

On August 25, 1942, the former Hawkeye hero was commissioned an ensign. He was given a three-week leave before returning to duty in Norfolk, Virginia. He spent the precious time off with his family in Adel, then it was on to Iowa City.

On, September 19, 1942, a beautiful autumn day, Nile Kinnick made his last appearance at the stadium that was eventually to bear his name. He attended the Hawkeyes' season opening football game against Washington University of Missouri (a 26-7 Iowa triumph) and was invited to watch from the press box.

When fans got word that he was in the press box, the crowd began chanting, "We Want Kinnick!" over and over. In a letter to his parents, he said he had not realized what the fans were saying until someone told him.

"I was hesitant to believe it, for I couldn't hear them, but when reassured I walked to the door and sure enough they were yelling just that. Wasn't it wonderful. Such a fine, spontaneous gesture! Certainly the people of Iowa have been good to me."

He waved to the crowd, and that night attended a party in a restaurant in nearby Tiffin, a popular hangout for Iowa sports boosters and athletes. He went to church Sunday morning, and took a trolley to Cedar Rapids to visit more friends. He also saw the movie, "Pride of the Yankees," starring Gary Cooper as baseball legend Lou Gehrig.

Two days later, he left Iowa City by train, never to return. He had entered the final phase of his young life.

In December of 1942, he was assigned to the aircraft carrier U.S.S. Lexington, one of 24 Essex-class carriers built during World War II. It would be his last home. After Norfolk, he was sent to Rhode Island, where he went aboard the giant ship. It was large enough to hold 5,000 men, and could have supported three football fields or one thousand cars on its main deck. He spent Christmas alone in the Boston area, and wrote home about how lonely he was and how much he missed Iowa. The following is a poem he wrote to his younger brother, George, on December 20, 1942, telling of his affection for Iowa in the winter.

"Oh, I long for Christmas back in Iowa,
Where the landscape is white with snow.
Where the ponds and rivers freeze,
And the north wind is sure to blow.

I want to slam down on my sled,
Cut a figure eight with my skates.
Do all the things I used to do.
Before we began to play for higher stakes.

Race out of the cold in by the fire,
Soon warm before the flickering blaze,
With popcorn to eat and stories to tell,
Who doesn't yearn for those wonderful days?

Christmas without cold and snow is not the same,
It's like a picture without a frame.

As bright and dedicated as he was, Nile found the art of flying difficult to grasp at times, yet in the long run was pleased that he passed all the tests. He gives his first hint of his feelings about working off a large ship on May 7, when he writes: "Carrier duty would be exciting, adventurous, full of action, requiring the utmost in skill and daring."

Though excited about the adventure of being a fighter pilot when he first began training, there is a sadness that permeates his writings. Several times he complains of the boredom of service life, and admits that he is feeling lowly, or somewhat depressed. It is abundantly clear that he dearly missed his family and friends, and the comfort and security of Iowa City.

In a letter dated February 24, 1943, he offered a keen evaluation of the potential conflicts of big government: "If the gov't continues to 'take over' more & more, who is going to be the arbiter in any complaints and disputes which arise? The tyranny and abuses of business and labor will then be present in the government itself and doubly hard to correct."

It was as if he was looking far into the future, when those issues would almost completely enflame the American political scene.

The Gulf of Paria is located between the island of Trinidad and the coast of Venezuela, in South America. After the long voyage from Rhode Island, down through the Panama Canal and out into the Caribbean Sea, the U.S.S. Lexington entered the Gulf of Paria on May 16, a date Nile noted in his diary. On June 1, he made his final entry. The statements were characteristic of the man, always eager to learn something new, always considerate of others.

"How I wish I could sing and play the piano," he wrote, and then added, "People must come before politics."

The very next day – on June 2, 1943 – Nile Clarke Kinnick, Jr., flew his Grumman F4F-4 Wildcat fighter plane off the deck on a training mission. The plane was a one-seater with a length of 29 feet, and a maximum speed of 325 miles per hour. It was 8:30 in the morning. About 80 minutes into the training flight, trouble was spotted. His roommate and close friend, Bill Reiter, had been flying alongside Kinnick for much of the exercise. He radioed over to Nile that his plane was leaking and they should return to the U.S.S. Lexington.

Nile radioed back to the ship, requesting permission to return. He was asked to try and wait while they cleared the takeoff and landing strip, reducing the danger risk of bringing back the plane to a crowded deck. He quickly agreed to keep the plane airborne, if possible. But a few minutes later, he was forced to make an emergency landing. It was, according to Reiter, a picture perfect landing in smooth water. He also said he saw Nile in the water, apparently free from the plane, but he was not signaling up to him.

A rescue boat was immediately dispatched and arrived at the scene within ten minutes, along with search planes. But no sign of Nile or the plane was seen. The rescue crews searched for several hours. To this day, no one can be certain what happened, though the prevailing opinion is that he must have struck his head on something, either in the plane or when thrown clear, and was rendered unconscious. He could have been connected to the plane through his rigging or in some other way. The plane sank in less than ten minutes, in all probability pulling Nile down with it.

The pride of Iowa, and one of America's brightest hopes, was gone forever.

Reiter was the only person who saw the plane go down; he wrote a letter to Nile's parents saying what a great friend Nile was and providing his opinion of the tragic accident. Sadly, Reiter, a handsome young man who was part of the foursome in Kinnick's flight group, was himself killed on September 5, 1943, in a night battle at Wake Island. He left behind a wife and young baby.

The decades have been extremely kind to Nile Kinnick's memory. He has passed from football hero to campus legend to icon. His fame has slowly spread across the nation, and shows up in special places from time to time – like in *LIFE* magazine, in 1999:

"The entire nation swooned over Kinnick," wrote E.J. McGregor. He then repeated the statement of a Boston Post reporter from the night of the Heisman banquet: "This country's okay as long as it produces Nile Kinnicks. The football part is incidental."

Iowa has produced many great leaders and wonderful men and women, but Nile Kinnick does seem to rise above the rest, somehow – just like in 1939, when he rose above Joe Louis, world heavyweight boxing champion, and Joe DiMaggio, superstar of the New York Yankees, to be named the Associated Press Male Athlete of the Year. DiMaggio hit .381 that year and Louis knocked out four challengers for his title, but the nation's sportswriters were so enthralled by Nile Kinnick and the gritty band of Hawkeye players known as The Ironmen that they placed Kinnick on a level above even the Yankee Clipper and the Brown Bomber!

Kinnick's football exploits were extremely important in setting a high standard for the coming generations of Hawkeye athletic teams. As Tait Cummins, one of the best-known sports announcers in Iowa history, once wrote, it was Kinnick, and his coach, that changed everything in Iowa City:

"One player and one coach filled an empty stadium with 52,000 paying customers. They retired all the debt and they started athletics out in a complete new era. (Iowa) has never been in the hole since, thanks to 1939 and Nile and Dr. Anderson."

Al Grady, the longtime sports editor of the Iowa City paper, was asked to appear on an ESPN special about Kinnick in 2000. During the taping, Grady began to reminisce about what Kinnick had meant to him as a young boy attending Iowa games, and as emotion overcame him, Grady broke down on camera.

Still, after so many years, one question lingers over the Iowa landscape, and it is this: How far would Nile Kinnick have traveled in life had not the war intervened?

"He told me one day in Iowa Falls that his goal was to be governor," said Frank Nye, a highly-regarded political writer during his years with the Cedar Rapids Gazette. "And he would have been a shoo-in eventually. That's the least he would have been. He's the kind of fellow who could have become President."

Erwin Prasse, who was his teammate all during their Iowa careers, labeled Kinnick a genius and thought he could have been a senator or president.

"I never met another person equal to Kinnick," Prasse told Ron Maly of the Des Moines Register in a 1989 interview. Prasse won nine letters at Iowa and went on to a long and successful business career in Illinois. *(31)*

Forest Evashevski, coach of the great University of Iowa teams of the 1950s, played at Michigan with Tom Harmon, the 1940 Heisman Trophy winner, and against Kinnick. He, too, felt that Kinnick's future was practically without limits, in just about any career he would have chosen.

"I wish every football player in the world could grow up to be like Nile

Kinnick," said Evy in 1981. "It would be a better world in which to live."

On October 30, 1990, Ronald Reagan returned to his hometown of Dixon, Illinois, for a visit. The editor of the city's newspaper was invited to be in a very small group of people that were going to meet the nation's 40th President.

"When I had a chance to shake the former President's hand, I had a question all prepared for him," said the editor. "'Mr. President, I know you used to broadcast Iowa football games in the 1930s, and so I wondered if you ever met Nile Kinnick?'

"Mr. Reagan stopped in his tracks, looked at me again, and smiled.

"'Noooo, I never did,' he said in that familiar voice. 'I was gone to California by the time Nile was playing at the university. But I wish I would have met him. He was quite a man.'"

And then the editor offered his own opinion of Nile Kinnick: "I've read a great deal about his life, and had he not died at the age of 24 on a training flight during World War II, I think he might have become someone very, very special.

"Mr. Reagan nodded and then added a line the editor said he will never forget: 'Yes, I agree. I think he could have been anything he wanted, maybe even President of the United States!'"

The former President of the United States said he thought Nile Kinnick might have become President of the United States. It's an opinion shared by many who knew him.

Because he has become such an icon for the entire state, it is easy to overlook the fact that Nile Kinnick was a flesh and blood person, with aspirations, hopes and dreams and disappointments like everyone else. Though born and raised in Adel, he had come to maturity and national acclaim in Iowa City, and harbored a deep affection for that city. In fact, he dreamed of returning there after the war, in some fashion or other.

The last letter he is known to have written contained a glowing endorsement of his love of Iowa City. It was received by Ceila Peairs at her home in Des Moines the day after it was announced that Nile had died. It was written May 31, 1943.

"Am so glad you could speak enthusiastically of your visit in Iowa City.

That little town means so much to me – the scene of growth and development during vital years – joy and melancholy, struggle and triumph. It is almost like home. I love the people, the campus, the trees, everything about it. And it is beautiful in the spring.

"Ah, for those days of laughter and picnics when the grass was newly green and about a grab and a half high. I hope your friend showed you through the Union, the Fine Arts Bldg., the Little Theater of which we are so proud. And I hope you walked off across the golf course just at twilight, and felt the peace and quiet on an Iowa evening, just as I used to do." *(33)*

It was so poignant, and so Nile Kinnick.

He was also, by many accounts, shy and somewhat introspective around others. Wallace Butler was a member of the Phi Kappa Psi fraternity when Nile joined in the fall of 1939, and he has several fond recollections of the man who was the biggest star on campus, and all across the state.

"I can't say I knew him well because he was so shy and reserved," said Butler, a retired lawyer who now lives in Las Vegas. "He was a nice, decent fellow, sharp as a whip, but very quiet. He never said much at all."

Butler was over six foot tall and weighed over 200 pounds, so he was assigned to "take care" of Kinnick in a frat initiation game in the living room, where the action got a bit rough. Butler didn't fare so well.

"We had a big battle in the living room. Because of my size, I was assigned to Nile and ran into him," said Butler with a chuckle. "He just took me out. I was on the floor in a second. Then he reached down to help me up."

Butler also recalled the time that Kinnick displayed his unusual strength.

"He braced his feet and held his arm out straight to the side and told me to hang from it," said Butler. "I said I didn't think he could hold me, but he said to grab his arm. I did, and lifted my feet off the ground, all my weight on his arm, and he held it out straight for several seconds. He didn't budge. Just try that some time! He was not very big, about five foot eight inches tall, but he was very strong for his size."

Kinnick was a natural athlete, from the time he was a young boy in Adel. Butler saw that aptitude first hand.

"I taught him how to play ping pong," said Butler, "and I guess I did a pretty good job, because about six months later, Nile won the university ping pong championship." *(34)*

Kinnick was an outstanding physical specimen, and Dr. Eddie Anderson once said his body was like steel or hard rubber. Kinnick proved his athletic ability after he joined the Naval Reserve. On January 23, 1943, he wrote in his diary about his performance in a test the week previous:

"The physical education instructors have given strength tests to all students the past few days …. my efforts …. eight feet and two inches standing broad jump, 31 back levers, 16 chin-ups, 40 push-ups for a total of 354 points – 80 points higher than anyone else – the instructors seem to think it is a pretty good mark to shoot at."

The shyness of his nature is also well documented. It even extended to the girls, according to Butler and several others who knew Kinnick well.

"He was very popular because he was 'big man on campus.' But did he ever date? No, not once, that I am aware of," said Butler. "He was too shy for that."

In 2005, Peg Nelson, living in Waterloo, recalled meeting Kinnick on campus shortly after she won the Miss Iowa crown. She was with a group of friends when she spotted him.

"I saw him near the Old Capitol and waved and he came over and said, 'Congratulations on winning Miss Iowa,'" Peg recalled. "I told him it was nothing like winning the Heisman Trophy and tried to talk to him about the trip to New York City and all of that, but he just waved it off and wanted to talk about my little contest.

"That's the way I remember Nile," she said, somewhat wistfully. "Just a wonderful young man, and more interested in talking about other people than himself." *(35)*

During his training in Kansas City, Kinnick had looked up a young lady, Merle McKay, who had attended Iowa for a while and was working in Kansas City while living with her parents. It is clear from his diary that he was smitten with her and enjoyed her company tremendously.

"Man, did I have a good deal this evening!" he wrote. "By far the best since

I have been in Kansas City. I am referring to my date with Merle McKay. She turned out to be just as comely, just as shapely and just as nice as I remembered her at Iowa ...."

Several weeks later, after more dates, he wrote: "Merle, what a fine looking girl. I wish to goodness I had called her sooner." When time came for him to leave Kansas City and report to his new station, near New Orleans, Kinnick wrote that it was difficult saying goodbye.

In 1974, Merle wrote a letter expressing her feelings about the brief time she spent with him in the winter of 1942-43. "Knowing Nile Kinnick is a highlight of my life .... It is a rare privilege to have dated a football hero of such national acclaim. Nile came into our house easily. Mother and Dad had the highest respect for him. My 12-year-old brother idolized him.

"Nile had a rather dry sense of humor – to this day I can picture the twinkle in his eye as he made some far out comment. Some times Nile and I would start talking and never find a stopping place. Nile was not loquacious .... I often chided him in his more quiet moods telling him he was truly an Ironman.

"But Nile was the type of person one could be with comfortably in silence, a rarity, I've found." *(36)*

Among his many admirers was Dr. James Van Allen, one of the most respected scientists of the 20th Century, and the man who discovered the Van Allen Radiation Belt encircling the earth. The physics building on the Iowa campus is named in his honor.

"I met him once," said Dr. Van Allen in 2004. "I was a freshman nobody .... and he was the biggest man on campus. He was walking by my dorm when I spotted him coming right toward me. I was kind of nervous even seeing him so I just sort of nodded and said hi. He stopped and asked me my name, where I was from, where I was living, and wished me good luck. I was amazed that he would stop to talk with a freshman when he was the star of Iowa City.

"I will never forget that moment," said Dr. Van Allen. (37)

In 1999, the Iowa City Press-Citizen newspaper ran a special 60th Anniversary special section on "Nile Kinnick and the Ironmen." Sports Editor Bryce Miller interviewed several men who had known Kinnick personally, including Dean Jones, 90 years old at the time.

Jones drove Kinnick to the train depot in 1939, when Nile left Iowa City for New York City and the Heisman Trophy banquet. Six decades later, Jones was still in awe of his famous friend.

"He was the kind of young man that you want your boys to grow up to be like," Jones told Miller. "But seldom do they – because he was the pinnacle.

"I don't think I've ever met anybody like him in my life. There are a lot of nice people in this world, but there's nobody like Nile Kinnick."

It is true that there has never been an Iowan quite like Nile Kinnick Jr. Would he have been a senator or even President of the United States?

"Oh, easy," said Wallace Butler. "There would have been no stopping him. He had a golden tongue, and was so very smart. Yes, that would have been very possible, knowing Nile."

Of course, we will never know for sure how far Nile Kinnick Jr. would have gone had it not been for his death on June 2, 1943, at the age of 24 years, 11 months and a few days.

But this we do know: Nile Kinnick loved his state, and set the bar for generations to come, teaching us who knew his story – through his life and through his death – what it means to be a winner at the highest level.

Nile Kinnick is the most honored and lionized football player in the history of the state. He ran away with every conceivable honor, back then in that fabled season of 1939. He was carried off the field on the shoulders of his teammates as the Iowa crowd went wild.

He set numerous Iowa records and some of them stood for over half a century. He was voted to the All-Time Iowa football team in 1989, and was also voted most valuable player of that team, garnering the most votes. He was selected the ninth greatest college football player of all time several years ago by *College Football News*, and was elected to the College Football Hall of Fame in its first year, 1951. Despite the fact he was out of athletics by the age of 22, *Sports Illustrated* magazine voted him the No. 3 top sports figure in Iowa history, behind Dan Gable and Bob Feller, both of whom had far longer careers in sports.

D.W. Stump, in his 1975 biography of Kinnick, wrote: "Nile loved his family, his university and his native land. Born to a pioneer family of distinction, the grandson of a governor, scholar, athlete without peer – he was all that could be expected of a cultural hero. His tragic death, in the line of duty, a month before his twenty-fifth birthday, stunned and disappointed a nation that was anticipating his leadership in its highest echelons for years to come."

Supreme Court Justice Wiley B. Rutledge captured the essence of Kinnick with the following words, written the year of his death:

"His feet were swift, his hands strong and sure, his eyes clear and far-sighted, his mind quick like the running of lightning from cloud to earth. Few men have had the grace and strength of body he possessed. He used it with miraculous effect upon the field of sport to the glory of his school and the pride of his state. Nile Kinnick will be remembered as long as there is an Iowa."

That's why he is still so relevant to Iowa citizens yet today. For many, Nile Kinnick is the young, dashing, articulate, athletic hero who his teammates carried off the field after the upset of mighty Notre Dame that sun-drenched autumn day in 1939; Nile Kinnick set the standard for what it means to live one's life to the very fullest, and to be an Iowan of the highest commitment and of the highest character. He was truly one of a kind, and we may never see his like again!

Dr. Virgil W. Hancher, president of the University of Iowa during Nile's time there, paid him a tremendous tribute when hearing of his death.

"His life until June 2 was as near perfection as anything I expect to see in my time here. The inspiration of his example has affected and will continue to affect his college generation."

Former Ironman teammate Bill Green said he broke down and wept when he heard of Nile's death. Later, he summed it up best with these words about his legendary friend: "… he exuded hope and confidence. He was a meaningful symbol to all of Iowa." *(38)*

Sadly, Nile Sr. had to endure the terrible tragedy of seeing all three of his sons, and his wife, die. His second son, Ben, also served in World War II, as a Marine pilot, and died in action in the South Pacific on September 17, 1944, some 16 months after Nile's passing. George, the youngest, passed away in 1987.

Frances, the mother of the three boys, died in 1966.

Nile Kinnick Sr. passed away on July 23, 1989 – outliving Nile, Jr. by 46 years. He was 96 years old at the time of his death.

Today, the memory of Nile's deeds and accomplishments live on in numerous ways. There is a stadium in Iowa City that bears his name, filled to capacity most football Saturdays in the fall when the Hawkeyes take the field. Nile Kinnick Stadium is a fitting tribute to a remarkable man who graced the Iowa landscape with his presence for twenty four years, a time that was extremely fulfilling but way too brief.

A larger-than-life statue of Nile greets visitors to the east side of the stadium that bears his name. The ten-foot tall statue shows him carrying books on his way to class, and sporting his letter jacket.

The University of Iowa Athletic Hall of Fame in Iowa City has an entire section dedicated to his memory. On display are his Heisman Trophy, one of his jerseys with the No. 24, numerous photos on and off the field, several signed letters that he wrote to friends and fans, and a football signed by Nile and other members of the 1939 All-Star team, including Coach Eddie Anderson.

The area in Adel where young Bob Feller and Nile Kinnick played on the same baseball team is named Kinnick-Feller Park in honor of the two hall of famers. It is the largest and oldest park in the city.

Kinnick is one of four athletes (the others being Gary Thompson of Roland, Dan Gable of Waterloo and Shawn Johnson of Des Moines) honored with a statute in the beautiful Hall of Pride building in Des Moines.

A high school on the U.S. Air Base in Yokosuko, Japan, is named for him. So is the main street leading into Adel, and there are plans to build a museum in his hometown to honor him.

"Nile Kinnick's name is still spoken throughout the Midwest with pride, adulation and sadness," wrote Scott Fisher in his book, *The Ironmen*. "His achievements on the field may be surpassed, but his combination of dedication, inspiration, and talent will forever remain an unattainable goal." *(39)*

"Don't Forget Nile Kinnick" was the headline on a newspaper column wrote in 2006 by Jim Donaldson, of the Providence Journal in Rhode Island:

"During the Memorial Day weekend, when many of us are thinking about our backyard barbecue with the family, we should have taken a few minutes to remember Kinnick, and the thousands of men and women who have given their lives in service to this country."

The ship that was his home the final months of his life went on to earn a sterling reputation during World War II. After Nile flew off its deck for the final time, the U.S.S. Lexington served longer and set more records than any other carrier in naval history. The Japanese were unable to sink it; due to that fact and because it had a blue hue to it when seen on the horizon, the Japanese called it "The Blue Ghost." Today, it is a National Historic Site and museum which serves as a memorial to the men and women of the American armed services. It is docked in the bay at Corpus Christi, Texas. Nearly 300,000 visitors walk up its gangplank ever year.

"Of course, we know who Nile Kinnick was and try to honor his memory here," said Judith Whipple, ship historian. "We don't know exactly where Nile lived during the time he was on board but we do know the general area that the pilots lived in."

Whipple can point out several spots where Kinnick would have spent time, including the "Ready Room," where pilots gathered for final instructions before each and every flight. Another pilot on the Lexington, Lt. Ardis Durham, Jr., mentioned in a letter to Nile's parents that Nile often brought books on economics and taxation to the "Ready Room" to read while waiting to be called to his plane. *(40)*

There are still six chairs in that room from the 1940s; Nile would have sat in one of them prior to his fateful flight. Whipple said plans are under way to build a small exhibit area on the ship for Kinnick in the near future.

In 2003, Richard Tosow, a University of Iowa graduate, announced he had found the remains of Kinnick's plane in 100 feet of water, right where the records from the Lexington said the plane went down. Tosow grew up in Omaha and knew Kinnick as a hero he greatly admired. He enlisted the support of several others, including Al Couppee, who had been on the 1939 team with Kinnick and also admired him tremendously.

"We knew exactly where to look," Tosow said. "We have the coordinates from the Lexington ship's log that gave details of the crash. We have a Global Positioning System unit. That's how we were able to get right to the location." *(41)*

Couppee went so far as to announce the goal was to have the plane restored and then given to the University of Iowa to put on display outside of Kinnick Stadium. But the plan evaporated when the small group ran into resistance from people who felt it was disrespectful to the memory of the legendary Hawkeye to disturb his remains.

Had he not died during World War II, it's very possible that Nile Kinnick would have lived well into his eighties, and been recognized as an Iowa treasure everywhere he went. He may not have become President of the United States, as Ronald Reagan suggested, but at the very least he would have been a governor, senator or captain of industry.

Nile was aware of the dangers of serving in the military during a war, just like Fred Becker had been in 1918. A month before he died, Nile wrote a letter to his parents about the path he was on:

"This task which lies ahead is adventure as well as duty and I am anxious to get at it. I feel better in mind and body than I have for ten years and am quite certain that I can meet the foe confident and unafraid. I have set the Lord always before me, because he is at my right hand. I shall not be moved."

Then he added this poignant reflection on the meaning of family and faith: "Truly we have shared to the full life, love and laughter. Comforted in the knowledge that your thought and prayer go with us every minute, and sure that your faith and courage will never falter no matter the outcome, I bid you au revoir."

We can only dream of what the world would have been like with Nile Kinnick in it for the past six decades. Like Fred Becker and Jack Trice, he left far before his time.

Johnny Bright:

"Drake's Shining Star"

"Bright was victim of one of college football's ugliest episodes, 50 years ago today. Bright was viciously slugged several times by the same Aggie defender long after the play developed. One of the right crosses broke Bright's jaw, effectively ending the college career of what might have been the nation's best player that year."

– *Blair Kerkhoff, Kansas City Star*

Johnny Bright:
An Offensive Machine

When Johnny Bright strolled onto the cozy Drake University campus in the fall of 1948, no one could have realized what was in store for the Des Moines university in particular, and the game of football in general. After his three-year varsity career wound up in 1951, Bright left a legacy of achievement that may never be matched at any college. Looking at the facts alone, one can make the case that Johnny Bright is not only the greatest football player to ever wear Drake colors, he may be the best football player to represent any Iowa college or university.

The dynamic, athletic young man from Indiana had it all, including a name that lent itself to visions of grandeur. And it is sad that today very few Iowa football fans even know who Johnny Bright was and what he once meant to Drake University and to the state as a whole.

Bright was born on June 11, 1930, in Fort Wayne, Indiana. His mother raised Johnny, his three brothers and a sister basically by herself, and times were tough. They lived in an old house with cracks in the walls that allowed the freezing air to seep into the rooms in the winter. The four boys shared two beds, while their sister often had to sleep with their mother. Early on, Bright discovered that most of the young men in the neighborhood wound up in the austere-looking factories, struggling to earn a meager living in the drudgery of monotonous work; he was determined not to fall into that trap.

Young Bright was diligent in his class work and excelled in athletics of all sorts. He starred in football, basketball, track and field and even softball while attending Fort Wayne's Central High School. He was a hard-hitting defensive player and offensive whirlwind in football and, though just five feet and ten inches tall, was able to dunk a basketball. In track, Bright was a terrific sprinter and a record-setting pole vaulter. He was an overpowering pitcher in softball and could hit the ball out of the park with ease. He even participated in an after-school boxing program.

Along with his superb athletic skills, Bright had a pleasing personality that made him popular with both his teachers and his classmates. It was an attribute that would serve him well all the rest of his life, especially as he grappled with racism on various levels.

"While it could have been easy for Johnny to earn the envy of his peers – he was so superior in his athletic ability – he developed a positive charisma," wrote Warrick Lee Barrett in a biography of Bright. "He had a kind and playful nature that few people could fail to recognize." *(42)*

Central High was an Indiana state power in both football and basketball during Bright's starring years, and he was the catalyst. His football team made it to the state finals, and so did the basketball team. The track squad was one of the best in the state, as well. After a sensational athletic career, he graduated from high school in 1947 but was largely ignored by college football coaches.

"In this day and age he would have been heavily recruited," said Paul Morrison, the longtime sports information director at Drake, in 2008, "but 65 years or more ago African-American athletes were not in demand like they are today. Several Big Ten schools, including his home state of Indiana University, had no interest in John." One college official reportedly even made the statement that the school already had enough black players there.

Bright enrolled at Michigan State University, but left after only a couple of weeks. He didn't feel comfortable on the large East Lansing campus and was looking for a smaller school where he thought race and social status would not be an issue. The name Drake kept popping up, so he began to listen to advocates of the private institution, which had an enrollment of just under 5,000 students at the time.

Much of the credit for discovering Johnny Bright goes to Russ Cook, Drake's athletic director, and to Tom Deckard, the track coach. When he was stationed at Great Lakes Naval Base during World War II, Cook heard stories of the sensational high school athlete down the road in Fort Wayne, Indiana. Since Cook was acquainted with Bright's high school coach, he talked to him about Drake as a possibility for Bright.

As a native of Indiana, Deckard also kept in contact with associates back home who told him about the Fort Wayne star. Between Cook and Deckard, Bright was convinced to give Drake a try. It was a decision that would pay huge dividends for the Bulldogs and would make Bright a household name across the state of Iowa for three years.

In the fall of 1948, Bright and a friend, Ned Brenizer, who also played sports at Central High School, took a train from Fort Wayne to Chicago, and then to Des Moines. It would take a year, but the stage was set for an amazing story.

Though he originally intended to participate in just basketball and track, Johnny wanted to try football as well. Freshmen weren't eligible for varsity competition in 1948, and Bright spent his first year at Drake making the adjustment to college and settling into campus life. But in 1949, he exploded onto the national football scene.

"The understanding was that I was being recruited mainly for those two sports," Bright told Maury White of the Des Moines Register, when being inducted into the newspaper's sports hall of fame in 1970. "I said I'd come providing I could also try out for the football team."

"Bright not only made the football team but he MADE Bulldog football for three brilliant years ...." added White. *(43)*

Bright wasn't the only newcomer to the Drake football program in 1949. Warren Gaer arrived as the head coach after building a strong program at Pepperdine College in California the previous six years. Gaer had been captain of the 1934 Drake team and was a proponent of the single wing offense, which was perfect for a player with the talents of Johnny Bright. It was an offense that focused on getting the ball into the hands of an exceptionally gifted athlete who could both run and pass.

At nineteen years of age, Bright stood six foot tall and weighed 190 pounds of solid muscle, large for a running back. He was blessed with explosive athletic skills. Taking the field for the 1949 season, Bright showed fans what was to come that season with a standout performance in the season opener against South Dakota State, a 49-0 Bulldog romp.

In Bright's first college game, he ran for 116 yards on 11 carries and passed for 134 more. He scored twice, on runs of 10 and 53 yards, the latter effort called "brilliant" in the Bulldog annual.

The next week, against Emporia State Teachers College of Kansas, some 9,000 fans saw Bright score touchdowns on runs of 59 and 50 yards, and pass to Tom Bienemann for a 72-yard score. Bright romped for 174 yards on just 11 carries, averaging an amazing 16 yards per run in the 42-0 triumph.

In the third game, Drake whipped Bradley 17-7 without a score from Bright, but he ran for 163 yards. He scored three touchdowns and passed for another in the fourth game, a 48-6 triumph over South Dakota University.

Drake was sporting a 4-0 record when it journeyed south to take on Oklahoma A&M in a Missouri Valley Conference showdown in Stillwater, Oklahoma. Bright was held to just 27 yards rushing but managed 113 yards in the air, for a total output of 140 yards. The Aggies proved too powerful and prevailed, 28-0. The game was uneventful in terms of racial problems, but two years later the game between the two conference powerhouses would rock the entire world of sports.

The Bulldogs rebounded the next Saturday at home with a 27-14 win over St. Louis University as Bright threw for two touchdowns and picked up 133 yards rushing on 25 carries. In the seventh game of the season, he passed for two more touchdowns in a 13-13 tie with tough St. Mary's in San Francisco, California. That sent the Bulldogs into their big rivalry with Iowa State College sporting a 5-1-1 record.

Playing before a crowd of 20,000 at homecoming, Drake suffered a 21-8 loss to the Cyclones as the visitors managed to keep the Bulldogs out of the end zone most of the day. Bright rushed for 159 yards but wasn't able to cross the goal line. The crowd is still the largest ever to witness a Drake home game, with 18,000 in the stands and nearly 2,000 more sitting in bleachers on the west side and in the end zone.

In the season finale, Drake defeated Wichita 7-6, as Bright was limited to 52 yards rushing. But he tossed a 20-yard touchdown pass to Bobby Clark for the only Bulldog score of the game.

Drake had compiled a 6-2-1 record – and its sophomore star led the entire nation in total offense with a perfect balance of passing and rushing. For the season, Bright ran for 975 yards and threw for 975, a total of 1,950 yards of offense. The Bulldog sensation was named first team All-Missouri Valley Conference and the stage was set for an even bigger year in 1950.

With the football season in the books, Bright turned his attention to basketball and played on a Bulldog team that posted a 14-12 record. Just as in football, Bright was the only black athlete on the squad. He didn't see much action but did earn a letter and was touted at the end of the season as someone who would make a difference in the next two years.

But Bright's destiny was already centered on football. He had made a huge impact in 1949 and was a marked man as the 1950 season began.

"He was big, strong, fast and durable," wrote White, a former Drake star himself before turning to sportswriting. "Coach Warren Gaer put his ace deep in a spread formation called the BURP (Bright, Run or Pass). It was a horrible name but a beautiful sight." *(44)*

His second football season was more of the same – much more! He rushed for 1,232 yards and passed for another 1,168, setting a new NCAA record for total offense with 2,400 yards. He averaged 266.7 per game, which was another NCAA record.

Not only that, but Bright became the first football player in the state to rush for more than 1,000 yards in a season. The Cyclones didn't see their first 1,000 yard rusher until George Amundson in 1971, some twenty years later. The Hawkeyes did not have a runner go over that magic mark until Dennis Mosley in 1979, nearly three decades after Bright accomplished the feat. Those facts offer more evidence of how far ahead of his time Johnny Bright actually was.

The 1950 season began with a 7-0 win over Denver University, as Bright ran 32 yards for the game's only touchdown. He finished with 107 yards on the ground and another 47 in the air for a total of 154 yards.

The Bulldogs dominated Emporia State in the second game, 47-6, as Bright scored twice on the ground and threw for two more scores. He finished the game with 223 yards of total offense.

The Drake junior exploded the following Saturday against South Dakota State with his best rushing effort ever. On the first play of the game, Bright dazzled the crowd with an 89-yard sprint for a touchdown, and scored twice more on runs of 29 and 17 yards. He connected on nine of ten passes for two more scores as the Bulldogs breezed to a 41-13 triumph. He finished the game with 246 yards on the ground in just 15 carries and added another 135 in the air for a total of 381 yards!

The Drake sensation was becoming the talk of the sporting nation. After pacing the entire country in total offense as a sophomore, he was running and passing at an even higher clip. Not even the big offensive stars of Notre Dame, Ohio State and Southern Cal could match the fireworks of the powerful and swift halfback playing in Des Moines, Iowa.

Oklahoma A&M invaded Drake Stadium the following week and the two teams battled to a 14-14 tie. Bright accounted for both of his team's touchdowns, the first coming on a 23-yard run and the second on a 54-yard pass play to Bob Binette.

Iowa State Teachers College was the next foe and the Panthers were overwhelmed by a Bright-led attack, 34-18. He scored on a 65-yard run and racked up 130 yards rushing and 262 passing, connecting on 17 of 24 passes. His day's work totaled 392 yards.

The following week, Wichita, sporting a 5-0 record, was able to hold Bright to just 173 total yards, his second lowest output of the entire season. He scored just once as the Bulldogs fell to the Shockers, 17-14. Years later, Wichita coach Jim Trimble found a new term with which to characterize Bright's powerful running.

"He epitomized what I thought was the ideal running back – the splatter type," said Trimble of the Drake star. "When he got rolling, he just splattered people."

The next Saturday, Bright threw for one touchdown in a 14-13 loss to Detroit, totaling 219 yards.

But the Iowa sensation saved his best performance for Bradley. He racked up 436 yards of total offense and was responsible for six touchdowns – three on the ground and three by passing as the Bulldogs pounded the visitors, 42-14. He had 186 yards rushing and 250 through the air, a stunning performance even from an athlete with his gaudy credentials.

Bright closed out the campaign by leading Drake to a resounding 35-21 win over Iowa State. He tore through the Cyclone defense on a 71-yard scoring run, and later powered over from the four-yard line with three Cyclones on his back. He wound up with four touchdowns and 168 yards on the ground and added another 61 through the air.

The Bulldogs finished 6-2-1 for the second straight year, outscoring their opposition by a 247 to 117 margin. Bright was a unanimous first team all-conference selection again and also began to earn some All-American mention, being named to the first team picked by INS (International News Service) and second team by the AP (Associated Press).

Bright was even being mentioned as the state's first serious Heisman Trophy candidate since Nile Kinnick won the top college award twelve years earlier. Johnny Bright had turned Drake University into one of the nation's most followed football programs!

In the summers between seasons at Drake, Bright kept busy with fast-pitch softball, and left his mark on that sport, as well. In 2009, Jim McGrew, a retired principal at Waverly High School, recalled playing against Bright one year in particular.

"He was outstanding, he probably had the fastest pitch of anyone in the state," said McGrew. "He played for an all-black team from Des Moines called Hot-N-Tots. They won the 1951 state tournament. It was a very popular team and Johnny Bright was the big star, of course.

"In the state championship game in Boone, the stands were filled to capacity, with cars parked all the way around the field. There were over 2,000 fans there. He was a big name, the big draw. Yes, indeed."

In the finals against Fort Dodge, Bright gave up just one hit and struck out ten men. He also batted clean-up, recording one hit and several walks in the game.

"His team won that game and went on to the regional championships, making it all the way to the finals," said McGrew. "But he couldn't play in the regional game because he had to be back at Drake for the start of football.

"There weren't a lot of black athletes in the fast-pitch game back then. Johnny Bright was well liked by other teams. He was a great guy, always with a big smile, he was confident but not cocky at all." *(45)*

In the fall of 1951, football fever was running hot and heavy on the Des Moines campus as the Bulldogs prepared for their third and final season with Johnny Bright at the helm. He had continued to mature during college and by his fourth year was a marvelous physical specimen.

"Inflation, of a muscular type, set in," wrote Maury White. "Called 'Panda' because of his bushy, black eyebrows, Bright had grown to a smidgen over 200 pounds, mostly in the arms and shoulders. His coat size went from 42 to 46 in two years.

"Arm tackles couldn't bring down the All-American back, and other type tackles often failed. His knees pounded foes; Bright's passing was slightly sidearm but highly effective.

"The stage was set for a sensational climax to one of the finest careers in college history. But tragedy was lurking just around the corner." *(46)*

Bright got off to a roaring start. He ran for 158 yards in 30 carries in the opener against Abilene Christian College as the Bulldogs posted a 19-7 triumph. He also passed for 104 yards. His total of 262 yards was 113 more than the entire Abilene Christian team.

He scored three touchdowns in a 20-7 win over Denver University in the second game, and connected on eight of 10 passes. He followed that up with another huge game in Peoria, Illinois, romping for 192 yards on 20 carries in a 20-14 triumph over the Bradley Braves.

The next weekend, Iowa Teachers invaded Des Moines on a rainy day and was destroyed by both the mud and the Bulldogs.

"John Bright and his crew did not disappoint the rain-ravaged crowd although he played only 15 minutes total," reported the Drake yearbook. "In those 15 minutes, John added 261 yards to his personal total, passing the three-mile mark – 5,388 yards – in his college career.

"Before Coach Gaer removed Bright and loaded the game with freshmen and sophomores, John gave the crowd a thrill that made up for the weather. He took a direct pass from center on his own 19 and took off on his familiar wide sweep of right end. Behind sparkling blocks, John dashed into the Tutors' secondary and over to the west sidelines to outdistance Teachers' safety man, Leland Crew, a quarter miler on the Panthers' track team." *(47)*

For his brief time in the contest, Bright accounted for five touchdowns, three on the ground and two in the air.

The Titans of Detroit University were up next and the Bulldogs were riding high at 4-0. On the day before the game, the Indiana native was honored with "Johnny Bright Night," as Des Moines Mayor A. B Chamber issued a proclamation on his behalf and Governor William S. Beardsley autographed a football that was to be used in the game the next day. Since Bright had gained some three miles of yardage in his career to date, a relay team was set up to take the football three miles – from the State Capitol building through the downtown and over to the Drake campus.

Nearly two thousand fans gave him a standing ovation when he walked into the Drake Fieldhouse to conclude ceremonies. He was presented the Al Couppee Athletic Achievement Award by sportscaster Al Couppee, who played on the 1939 University of Iowa "Ironman" team with Nile Kinnick. The plaque carried the inscription, "In recognition of his outstanding record as a member of the Drake University football team, for sportsmanship displayed and for his contribution to the game of football itself."

The next day, Bright treated the 13,000 fans to one of his best efforts in a Drake uniform. He scored four touchdowns and totaled 287 yards as the Bulldogs chewed up the visiting Titans, 28-6.

Going into the sixth game of the season, Drake was unbeaten and Bright was leading the nation in total offense for the third straight year! He was being mentioned as a leading candidate for the Heisman Trophy and pro scouts across the land were drooling with anticipation of his entry into the National Football League the next fall.

It looked like the Bright Express was unstoppable. But a team of Aggies and a player named Smith were lying in wait.

The Bulldogs traveled to Stillwater, Oklahoma – the site of the Great Land Rush of 1889 – with high expectations. They knew the Aggies would be very tough to beat on their home field, but they had gained considerable confidence from a solid winning streak and from knowing they had the nation's top offensive weapon at their disposal. So far, Bright had rolled up 821 yards rushing and 1,349 yards passing – and he was once again leading the country in both categories!

But it didn't take long for the game to erupt in controversy, one that would burn like a bed of hot coals for several months and then simmer for nearly half a century!

Oklahoma A&M was one of the last colleges to integrate its campus and athletic teams. When Drake played there two years earlier, there had been no racial tension in the game, but Bright was not allowed to stay in the motel with the rest of the team. Drake had found housing for him with an off-campus family.

In a speech given in 2008 at the dedication of Johnny Bright Field at Drake, Paul Morrison made the following observations: "As an aside, I should inform you that Johnny Bright and other black athletes from northern schools like Drake were not able to stay with the team at their hotels in places like Wichita, Tulsa and North Texas State. We made special arrangements for them at private homes, many of them church members." *(48)*

Bright had been a relatively unknown sophomore and was not able to make much of a difference in the 1949 game, which the Aggies won handily. But in 1951, the climate had changed. Drake was a real contender and Bright was a huge star. The week before the game, there was a considerable amount of talk in Stillwater about stopping Bright, or even forcing him out of the game. Whether or not it was racial in nature or simply the desire to stop a great athlete is hard to determine. Some who were heavily involved are not in total agreement, and even Bright himself seems to have changed his view over the years.

Once the game began, it didn't take long to see what was brewing. Wilbanks Smith, a husky Oklahoma A&M defensive tackle who also was a member of the Aggie wrestling team, tore into Bright without reservation. On the very first Drake play from scrimmage, Smith delivered a late blow that decked Bright. Staggering back to his feet, on the next play Bright managed to throw a 61-yard down touchdown pass to halfback Jim Pilkington, but he had to leave the field moments later, dazed and shaken.

Bright returned shortly after to find more of the same treatment. In the first seven minutes of play, Smith hit him late three times, with no penalties called. All were blows delivered to the face. It was an era without facemasks, and Bright was virtually unprotected. Even worse was that two of the blows came after Bright had handed the ball off or thrown it, and the final one came when he was lying on the ground after being gang tackled.

After the third attack, Bright left the game and never returned. Drake lost the game, 27-14. In less than one quarter of play, Bright had 14 yards rushing and 61 passing, marking the first time in his collegiate career that he finished with less than 100 yards of total offense.

The results raged far beyond the narrow confines of a football field. The referees never penalized A&M for what seemed flagrant fouls to many observers. A series of photos taken by Des Moines Register staffers John Robinson and Don Ultang showed what really happened on the first controversial play, and it was extremely disturbing. The blow from Smith was thrown long after Bright had handed the ball to fullback Gene Macomber, and deep behind the line of scrimmage.

"Wilbanks Smith, disregarding the movement of the play, had eyes for Bright only and three times crashed through the Drake line, and laying John out with what has been called 'illegal blocks,' but what from motion pictures of the game looked more like old-fashioned uppercuts to the jaw," said the Drake annual of 1951. "Thus began one of the biggest scandals ever to hit the Missouri Valley Conference." *(49)*

The series of events became known as "The Johnny Bright Incident" and started a firestorm among the nation's sports reporters and fans. The repercussions were felt around the country and endured for nearly half a century. The photos by Robinson and Ultang were displayed in many newspaper around the country. *LIFE* and *Time* magazines also ran the photos, and the Des Moines pair won a Pulitzer Prize for news photography.

Sec Taylor, the longtime sports editor of the Des Moines Register, wrote a column saying that Smith's uniform should be fumigated and hung up as an example of the worst aspect of college athletics. *LIFE*, the nation's most popular magazine at the time, called the action "the year's most glaring example of dirty football."

Macomber, the man Bright handed the ball to on that fateful play, told Blair Kerkhoff of the Kansas City Star in a 2001 article that he was in a barbershop in Stillwater the morning of the game. "They told me Johnny wasn't going to finish the game," said Macomber. *(50)*

Jack Jennett was a junior lineman on the 1951 team who went on to a successful career as head track coach at the University of Northern Iowa. He has no doubt that the incident was racial in nature, through and through.

"We couldn't even stay in a motel down there because of having a black player," said Jennett in 2010, "and wound up staying in the dorms. One of our coaches, Boots Stewart, said he had been watching films of the Aggie games before our game and noticed that Smith didn't even play in those games. He thought he was put in against us just to take care of Johnny."

Even after the hits, "Johnny didn't want to come out of the game but the trainer made him," said Jennett. "We were really upset when we saw what happened during the game and played as tough as we could the rest of the way. I remember waiting in the train depot after the game, ready to go back home. We were all sitting in a circle and Johnny was there, his jaw wrapped or wired to take the pressure off. The guy running the depot came over and told Johnny he couldn't sit in that area, as there was a separate area for blacks.

"John just looked at him and said, 'If you're man enough to move me, go ahead and try.' That was the end of it. The guy just turned around and walked away." *(51)*

Bright – and Drake – was never the same the remainder of the season. He had a tooth removed so he could be fed through a straw and his jaws were wired together. He missed the next game, sitting forlornly on the sidelines with his jaw wired shut, forced to watch his team sputtering on offense in a 13-0 loss to Iowa State. But, amazingly, he was back in the lineup on November 3 against Great Lakes.

"Two weeks after the ravaging Oklahoma A&M game, Johnny Bright, 11 pounds under his normal weight and weakened by a liquid diet, returned to limited duty and led his mates to a 35-20 victory over the sailors from Great Lakes," reported the Drake annual. "Wearing a specially built mask, Bright passed for two touchdowns, ran for another and wound up with a 204-yard total." *(52)*

However, his jaw was re-broken in the Great Lakes contest and Bright sat out the final game of his career, a 14-7 loss to Wichita.

Still, he was named first team All-American by the American Football Coaches Association and earned a second-team All-American berth by UPI (United Press International). He was honorable mention All-American in the AP listing and wound up fifth in the balloting for the Heisman Trophy. Only Dick Kazmaier of Princeton, Hank Lauricella of Tennessee, Babe Parilli of Kentucky and Bill McColl of Stanford attracted more points from the nation's voters.

Paul Morrison became the school's sports information director in 1946 and has seen well over 650 Bulldog football games, including every game Bright played at Drake. He said not only was Bright the best athlete the school ever had, he was far more.

"Great is an overworked word …. suffice it to say that Johnny Bright was that and more. He was a very unusual person. He was very popular on campus. He was nice and pleasant, and very personable. He was the type of person that would be a nice addition to any group of people you'd want to assemble, friendly and talkative.

"He was just an outstanding individual and had a lot of friends on campus. We kept up a correspondence for many years after he left Drake." *(53)*

Jennett also remembers Bright as a friendly person, if somewhat shy around people he didn't know well.

"I was a pulling guard and he was so dang fast he told me he'd run up my back if I wasn't moving fast enough," said Jennett. "I told him once if he continued to do that I'd leave a big hole in the line. We were always joking with each other; we got along really good. For the guys that knew him, he was great. He wasn't egotistical at all about all his accomplishments.

"Johnny was captain of the 1951 team and I was captain of the 1952 team. He sent me a letter and said, 'Remember when you are saying something to the team to make sure they understand what it is you are saying.' That was good advice, and something Johnny believed in, making sure others knew what he meant."

One day, Jennett also discovered first hand what a great pitcher Bright was.

"We were both pole vaulters and we were practicing in the Drake fieldhouse when he said he wanted to practice pitching for awhile. He asked if I would catch him and I said sure. He was whipping them in pretty good and then said, 'Get ready, here comes my drop ball.'

"I couldn't believe it. The ball came in and dropped so fast it hit my thigh. He did it again, hitting my other thigh. I took off the glove and said that was it, I was done catching him. The way he could make the ball drop like that was really something." *(54)*

Another popular Drake student at the time was Bob Ray, one of the most respected alumni in the school's rich history. He earned a bachelor's degree in business in 1952 and a law degree in 1954, and went on to a long and distinguished career in both politics and in business. He spent fourteen years as governor of Iowa, from 1969 to 1983, and even served as President of Drake University in 1998.

"I remember Johnny very well," said Ray from his Des Moines office in 2010. "He was heavily involved in athletics, of course, so we didn't bump into each other a lot but I do remember talking with him on several occasions and being very impressed. He was a warm and wonderful person; I've never come across anyone who didn't speak very highly of Johnny Bright. He was a great ambassador for sports and for Drake University."

Because he was president of the Student Faculty Council – the highest student office on campus – Ray was a member of the committee that was selected to deal with the Oklahoma A&M incident and eventually voted to leave the conference.

"I didn't see the game in person but was involved with the decision about protesting to Oklahoma A&M. What was so disappointing was that Oklahoma A&M took no responsibility for what happened. Had it not been for those photos taken by the Des Moines Register, the whole episode might have been ignored. We felt an example had to be made." (55)

Aggie coach J. B. Whitworth originally would not acknowledge that the play was illegal or dirty, and when the Missouri Valley Conference refused to take any disciplinary action, Drake resigned from the conference. In support of Drake, Bradley also pulled out but both returned several years later when Oklahoma A&M left to join the Big Eight Conference.

The longstanding rift finally came to an official end on September 28, 2005, when Oklahoma State President David Schmidly wrote an official letter of apology to Drake President David Maxwell, who had contacted him with a suggestion that they work together to end the matter. Schmidly said the incident "was an ugly mark on Oklahoma State University and college football and we regret the harm it caused Johnny Bright, your university and many others. Our desire is to keep this chapter behind us and move our two great universities forward."

Ironically, Morrison recalls that Bright didn't appear bitter about the Stillwater game.

"He just took it in stride," said Morrison. And the Drake athletics expert has his own views on the incident.

"I'm one of those who don't think it was entirely racial in nature," said Morrison. "He played down there in 1949 with no problem. But two years later, he was big news and a national figure. We were tied with them in the conference; they felt they had to get him out of the game. That's what it was all about, in my opinion." *(56)*

In 1980, three years before he died, Bright expanded on his feelings about both the game and the perpetrator.

"There's no way it couldn't have been racially motivated," he told the Des Moines Register. "What I like about the whole deal now, and what I'm smug enough to say, is that getting a broken jaw has somehow made college athletics better. It made the NCAA take a hard look and clean up some things that were bad." *(57)*

Because of the incident, facemasks were added to helmets and it became an infraction that demanded removal from the game if one player blatantly slugged another. Johnny Bright had once again made a major impact on the game he loved.

He added that he was "null and void" in his feelings toward the Aggie player. "The thing has been a great influence on my life. My total philosophy of life now is that whatever a person's bias and limitation, they deserve respect. Everyone's entitled to their own beliefs." *(58)*

After graduating from A&M, Smith embarked upon a long career in marketing with Exxon and today lives quietly with his wife in Kingston, Texas. His hometown of Mangum, Oklahoma, has a web site and lists him among the town's notables, and briefly mentions the October 20, 1951, game which made him a notorious figure in the eyes of many football fans around the country.

But memories of the incident lived on for half a century. It was resurrected in 2001 by a number of writers.

"Bright was victim of one of college football's ugliest episodes, 50 years ago today," wrote Blair Kerkhoff in the Kansas City Star. "Bright was viciously slugged several times by the same Aggie defender long after the play developed. One of the right crosses broke Bright's jaw, effectively ending the college career of what might have been the nation's best player that year." *(59)*

That same year, Adam Buckley Cohen wrote a story for the Los Angeles Times. He quoted Drake players as being so angry after Bright left the game that they sidelined three A&M running backs and, according to Drake safety Joe Sotelo, "just murdered their quarterback – absolutely demolished him – in retaliation. It was a rough, dirty day. Physically, we gave as much as we took." *(60)*

Cohen also contacted Wilbanks Smith for the story. The former Aggie told him, "Race had nothing to do with what happened that day."

By the end of his career, Bright owned twenty Drake records. In addition,

Johnny Bright: *"Drake's Shining Star"* 131

Left: **Johnny Bright shows the agility that he combined with power running to make him the nation's most potent offensive weapon during his three-year career at Drake University.**

Below: **Johnny Bright blasts into defenders from Abilene Christian in his senior year. Bright ran for 262 yards as the Bulldogs crushed the Texas school, 19-7, in the 1951 season opener.**

(Photos courtesy of Drake University Athletic Department)

Weighing 210 pounds his senior year, Bright was one of the nation's leading power runners, as the Bradley Braves found out (above) in their 1951 game. Bright scored two touchdowns in the Bulldogs' 20-14 victory.

Handsome and gregarious, Johnny Bright brought national attention to Drake University and Des Moines during his four years there.

In one of the most amazing photos in the history of college football, Johnny Bright takes a vicious forearm smash to the face from an Oklahoma A&M player named Wilbanks Smith at the outset of the October 20, 1951, game in Stillwater, Oklahoma. The blow came after Bright had handed the ball off to one of his teammates and was nowhere near the action. Even though it was a flagrant violation of the rules, no penalty was assessed and Wilbanks slugged Bright two more times during the first quarter, forcing him from the game with a broken jaw. This photo is the final one in a sequence taken by Des Moines Register photographers Don Ultang and John Robinson, and appeared in newspapers all over the country. The photographers won a Pulitzer Prize for their work. (Photo by John Robinson and Don Ultang. Copyright 1951, The Des Moines Register and Tribune Company. Reprinted with permission)

Johnny Bright shows the tight wires that were used to restrict his jaw movement after the Oklahoma A&M game. Bright was a leading candidate for the Heisman Trophy prior to the incident, but missed two of the next three games. He was limited to a liquid diet for a month.

(Photos courtesy of Drake athletic department.)

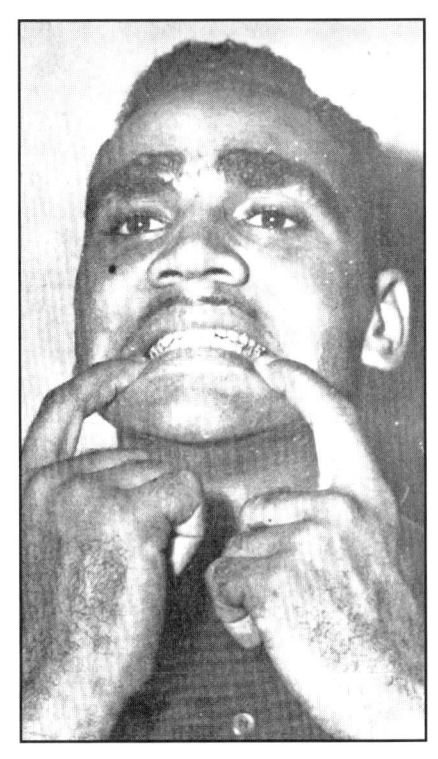

The week after the Oklahoma A&M game, Johnny Bright sat on the sidelines while his teammates lost to the Iowa State Cyclones. Bright missed the entire game but came back to play sparingly the next week and reinjured his jaw.

Johnny Bright: *"Drake's Shining Star"*

Although he saw action in most of the Bulldog basketball games his sophomore year, Bright (in photo at right) gave up the sport at season's end to concentrate on football and studies. He also was a standout softball pitcher during the summers for a Des Moines fast-pitch team.

Wearing uniform number 18, Bright poses with Drake pal Ned Brenizer at the start of the Bulldog season. Brenizer came to Drake with Bright from Fort Wayne, where they had been high school teammates.

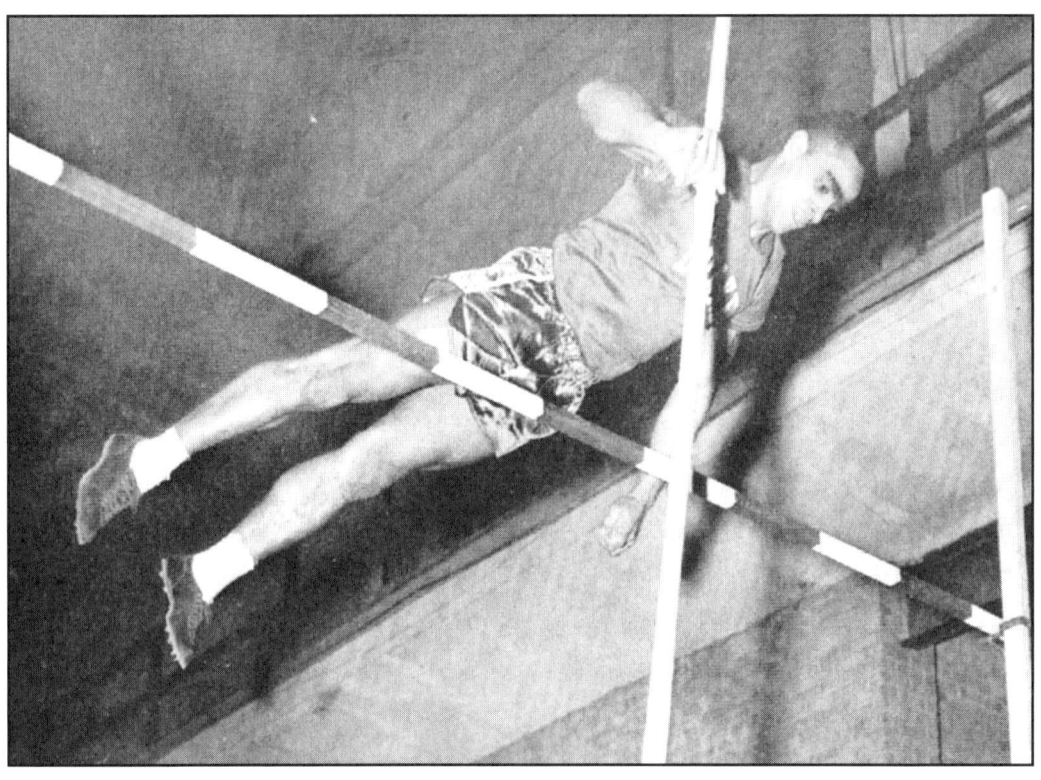

In addition to playing football and basketball as a sophomore, Johnny Bright participated in track. He was an exceptional pole vaulter (top) and sprinter.

(Photos courtesy of Drake athletic department.)

Johnny Bright: *"Drake's Shining Star"*

Although Bright missed out on the Heisman Trophy presented annually in New York City, the Drake star won the prestigious Swede Nelson Award handed out by the Boston Athletic Club. Nelson himself was on hand to present the trophy, given for outstanding sportsmanship, to Johnny.

Iowa sportscasters Al Couppee (center) and Bill Reilly present the Al Couppee Athletic Achievement Award to the Bulldog senior on Johnny Bright Night prior to the Detroit University game. Couppee was a starter on the 1939 Iowa team with Nile Kinnick. That night, 13,000 fans saw Bright gain 287 yards passing and rushing.

One of the league's top stars of all time, Johnny Bright was featured on several card sets sold in Canada.

During a sensational twelve-year career in the Canadian Football League, Johnny Bright won many honors. Here he stands with the trophy that he won for being named the CFL's most valuable player in 1959.

his 64 touchdowns and 236 career yards per game were NCAA records at the time. He had accounted for 5,983 yards in total offense, another national record, which included 3,134 rushing in 513 attempts. He averaged 6.1 yards per carry, still one of the best figures in college history.

His NCAA record for most touchdowns stood for 15 years, until 1966 when quarterback Virgil Carter of BYU scored 68 touchdowns. Bright's total offense record stood until that same year when Carter set a new mark of 6,354.

During his career, Drake teams went 6-2-1, 6-2-1 and 7-2 for an overall 19-6-2 record. It was the "brightest" football era in the 120-year history of the college.

After the season, he was given the Swede Nelson Award by the Boston Athletic Club, its version of the Heisman Trophy awarded by the New York Athletic Club. The Nelson Award was given annually to a college football player who "demonstrates a high esteem for the football code and exemplifies sportsmanship to a high degree." It was a wonderful recognition of the type of athlete, and person, that Johnny Bright had become in the eyes of the nation.

Bright was selected to play in both the Hula Bowl and the East-West Shrine Game, and then began contemplating a professional career. Though he was picked in the first round of the NFL draft by the Philadelphia Eagles, he gave considerable attention to the Canadian Football League (CFL) as well.

The CFL, though far less known in the States, had been in existence in various forms since the 1930s (though the current name wasn't adopted until 1958) and consisted of eight teams, separated into two divisions of four teams each. At the end of the season, the top two teams battled for the Grey Cup, the CFL's version of the Super Bowl. In the decades when sports teams of all types survived mainly through gate receipts and ticket sales, the CFL was on a financial foundation similar to that of the NFL. But the advent of big television money in the 1970s changed all of that; America had at least ten times the television market of Canada and the finances between the two leagues changed dramatically from that point on.

But in the 1950s, the CFL paid as much as the NFL and, in some cases, even more in an attempt to lure top American college stars up north. Two Canadian clubs, Edmonton and Calgary, were pursuing Bright in hot fashion. A Calgary team official named Cecil Chesire came to Des Moines on three separate occasions to visit with Johnny, telling him that the team was prepared to tailor its entire offense around his talents.

The difference in the NFL and the CFL turned out to be primarily money. Philadelphia reportedly offered the Drake star $8,000 a year while Calgary came up with $12,500. The gap in the two offers – and the fact that Calgary seemed genuinely interested in building its team around him – swayed John to go north. There might have been another less obvious reason.

Perhaps the memory of his problems in Stillwater, Oklahoma, was a factor. Many years later, Bright expressed his concern about how he would be treated in the NFL.

"I would have been their first Negro player," he said. "There was a tremendous influx of Southern players into the NFL at that time, and I didn't know what kind of treatment I could expect." *(61)*

It was just four years after Jackie Robinson had broken the color barrier in major league baseball and had suffered some terrible abuse from opposing players and fans alike. The country was still rife with racial prejudices. In Canada, the situation was much different for African-American athletes, who were treated with more respect and dignity.

Bright had also been involved in an ugly incident on campus during the fall of his senior year, according to author Warrick Lee Barrick in his book, *Johnny Bright, Champion*. Warrick told how a woman that Bright was dating had been accosted in a wooded area of campus during "Haunt Week." Several young men from a fraternity dressed up in sheets and hoods as Ku Klux Klan members in a Halloween prank that got out of hand. Walking through the spot after football practice, Bright saw his lady friend in trouble and rushed to her aide, scattering the troublemakers with a few punches.

Bright was so angry, according to Warrick, that he went to Coach Gaer and demanded that he do something or Bright would not play any more sports that year. Gaer reported the incident to the President of the University, who called in the culprits and made them publicly apologize. He also suspended the fraternity from various activities that year. *(62)*

Once his decision was made to play in Canada, Bright lost no time in showcasing his vast skills. As a member of the Calgary Stampeders, he played both ways, as a linebacker and fullback. His first season, 1952, he led the team and the Western Conference of the league with 815 yards rushing. The second season he was plagued by a series of nagging injuries, including a shoulder problem that continued to slow him down in 1954. Apparently, Calgary officials felt he was injury prone and midway through his third season traded him to Edmonton, the other CFL team that had wanted him back in his Drake days.

He soon got healthy and played 11 more years in the CFL. Edmonton used him strictly as a linebacker the first year, 1954, and then he played both ways for two years and was on offense the remaining eight seasons. In 1956, he set the Grey Cup rushing record with 171 yards in the Eskimos' 50-27 championship victory over Montreal.

The Bright train continued to operate at full steam for the next eight seasons. As one of the few athletes of that era to employ serious weight training methods, he continued to improve his power and strength in the off season.

In 1957, he rolled up eight straight 100-yard rushing games, finishing the season with 1,679 yards and the CFL rushing title. The following season, he upped the yardage to 1,722 and won the rushing title again. He took his third straight rushing championship in 1959, with 1,340 yards.

After the 1957 season, Coach Frank Clair of the Eskimo Rough Riders was so impressed that he declared Bright the best fullback in all of pro football, including the NFL: "There isn't a better fullback in football. I include anyone in the National Football League, even Rick Caseres of the Chicago Bears." In 1956, Caseres led the NFL in rushing with 1,126 yards and in 1957 he was the most respected power runner in the entire league. *(63)*

Bright was named the top player in the CFL in 1959, the first black athlete ever so honored. When he retired in 1964, after 13 seasons, Bright owned a goodly portion of the CFL record book. He had rambled for 10,909 yards, more than any player in league history. He had five consecutive seasons of 1,000 yards or more and led the league four times in rushing.

In addition, the ex-Drake star ran for over 100 yards on thirty-six occasions, a CFL record at the time of his retirement. His career average of 5.5 yards per carry is the best in professional football history – including the NFL; the legendary Jim Brown is second with a 5.2 yard average and Barry Sanders ranks third at 5.0.

By playing in 197 consecutive games, Bright had proved his durability and his toughness as well as his skills. His Edmonton jersey number 24 (the same as Nile Kinnick had worn at Iowa) was retired in 1983, some 13 years after he was inducted into the CFL Hall of Fame. In 2006, Bright was named 19th on the list of the top 50 players in the history of the Canadian Football League.

Among his many fans are Bud Grant, one of the most successful and respected coaches in football history, and Jim Walden, who went on to a long career as a football coach in several American colleges, including head coach at Washington State and Iowa State University, where Jack Trice had played decades before.

Grant was head coach of the Winnipeg Blue Bombers for ten years and then moved to the NFL, where he served as head coach of the Minnesota Vikings for 18 years. His 290 wins ranks him third on the all-time professional football coaching list, behind only Don Shula and George Halas. He is a member of both the Canadian Football Hall of Fame and the Pro Football Hall of Fame in Canton, Ohio.

Grant was a three-sport star in college (at the University of Minnesota) and, like Bright, was a first round draft pick in the NFL.

"I was the No.1 draft choice of the Eagles in 1950 and John was their top pick in 1951," said Grant. "They took a double hit, I guess .… first me and then John Bright."

Grant said money was the deciding factor in his decision and he supposed it was with Bright, as well.

"I played pro basketball with the Minneapolis Lakers and also played with the Eagles for two years. The Eagles didn't want to pay me what I thought I was worth and Winnipeg made a better offer. In those days it didn't have to be a lot to make a difference."

Grant was making $7,500 with the Eagles after his second season and Winnipeg offered more, so he made the trek north. He immediately became a star in the Canadian Football League, on both offense and defense, and began coaching in 1956. He led the Blue Bombers to six Grey Cup appearances and four championships, and was named CFL Coach of the Year in 1965.

He played against Bright and also coached against him.

"John was very tough to tackle. He was a big back compared to most in the 1950s," said Grant. "He was about 215 pounds and he played even bigger. In Canadian football, the defensive line has to be a yard off the ball, unlike the NFL where the defense can crowd the line. Pop Ivy was the coach for Edmonton and he put Johnny about 12 yards off the line of scrimmage so by the time he hit the defense he was really moving.

"He was a terror – our biggest nemesis. They had another black running back named Rollie Miles and they were a real one-two punch. One thing Bright had going for him was his durability, that was one of his greatest attributes."

Grant and Bright also saw each other in the off-season, during celebrity basketball games. "He played tough but clean," said Grant. "He was a very good athlete and competitor."

Grant said Bright would have been a star in the National Football League, as well, if he had decided to go that route instead.

"We all could have played in the NFL back then," Grant said of the many American college stars that opted for the Canadian league. "When I came down to coach the Vikings, I could have brought 15 guys with me. Johnny Bright would have done very well in the NFL, just like many others." *(64)*

A native of Mississippi, Jim Walden was a gritty quarterback at the University of Wyoming a few years after Bright finished at Drake. Walden was drafted by the Denver Broncos in 1960 but, like Bright, chose the Canadian route and played three years there. In 1961, he was traded to Edmonton when their star quarterback, Jackie Parker, went down with an injury. He has many fond memories of Bright, on and off the field.

"I was brought in as quarterback when Jackie got hurt," said Walden. "Parker was really great, like the Johnny Unitas of the CFL. Edmonton had a really high-powered offense and Johnny Bright was a big part of that, for sure. He was a truly great football player. He ran straight up and, man, he really socked you when he got rolling!

"I don't know why we hit it off so well, John and me, but we did, right from the start. I was a guy from the Old South, Mississippi, who wound up in Wyoming, and John got a kick out of that.

"Football players are kind of demented in their sense of humor, and some of us would tell Johnny in practice, 'Hey, look out, or I'll break that other jaw.' He would laugh and laugh, it was just a way to loosen up with him.

"Bright was a fun-loving guy who cracked jokes and liked to play pranks. He was just so much fun to be around. He was also a handsome guy, but had the darkest, heaviest eyebrows I've ever seen."

Walden also saw the serious side to Bright and admired that part of him as much as the football part, if not more.

"You know, he was a fascinating guy – I learned a lot from him. I loved his honesty. He made good sense in what he said. He talked about playing in Canada rather than the NFL. He said, 'I just want to go where I can play football and the race thing is not a factor. I've done my part of being a token, and I'm ready to move on from that.'

"We had long chats about that stuff and I really admired him for the approach he took."

The last time Walden saw Bright was at a coaching clinic in Vancouver in 1979. Walden was in the midst of a successful run as Washington State's head coach and was invited to be a guest speaker in Vancouver. The phone rang at his office prior to his departure; it was an old friend and Walden recalled the conversation with relish.

"He said, 'Hey, Walden, it's Bright.' Just like that. We hadn't seen each other in ten or fifteen years but it was like yesterday. He was coaching some high school football at the time and came to the clinic. We had a great, great time, just sitting and talking half the night."

Walden paused, then offered the following: "He was so well loved in Edmonton. Let me tell you this – whatever you heard about Johnny Bright that was good …. well, it was all true. And more. He was a wonderful person and I miss him." *(65)*

Several former Iowa Hawkeyes also went to Canada during the same era Bright played – including quarterback Ken Ploen, halfbacks Willie Fleming and Ray Jauch, and lineman Calvin Jones, one of the best players in Hawkeye history. After leading Iowa to a 35-19 triumph in the 1957 Rose Bowl, Ploen was signed by Bud Grant to play for Winnipeg and began a superb 11-year career in the CFL. He led the Blue Bombers to six Grey Cup title games and four championships.

Fleming and Jauch both did very well in Canada, but Jones's terrific potential was cut short by a plane crash in 1956. Jones was an All-American three straight years for Forest Evashevski and won the Outland Award in 1955 as the nation's top lineman. The plane crash occurred on December 9, 1956, and killed all 62 on board. Jones, who had just completed his first season in the CFL, was flying back to Winnipeg after playing in the league's All-Star game in Vancouver. Bright could have been on the plane if fate had not intervened.

Just a year later, in 1957, Bright and his family were visiting in Des Moines and he was interviewed by Tony Cordaro of the Des Moines Register.

"I played against Cal four times last year and he was good, real good," said Bright. "I was scheduled to play in that (all-star) game, but instead enrolled at Indiana. Who knows – if I had played in the game I might have been on the same plane." *(66)*

In its long history of sports, the University of Iowa has retired only two football jerseys – number 24, worn by Nile Kinnick, and number 62, worn by Calvin Jones.

All the time he was playing football Bright was looking ahead to his future in education and working with kids. He prepared himself well for a second career once his athletic days were over. He had told the Drake student newspaper back in 1951 that his primary interest was in helping young people.

"I want to get my master's degree with pro football paying the bills. I want to work with kids, do social work, work in recreation and coaching. I've always liked to work with kids and I know there are kids out there that, given positive contact at the right time, can make a needed turn-around in their lives."

During his last few years in the CFL, Bright began working on his masters at Indiana University. Once known as a prankster in the locker room, Bright took on a more serious demeanor the deeper he got into his career. He often was found reading text books in his spare time, and even picked up the nickname "Professor" among his teammates in Edmonton.

Bright and his wife, Lois, raised three daughters and one son. Johnny began teaching part-time in 1957, the year he moved his family to Edmonton, and he became a Canadian citizen in 1962. He retired from football after the 1964 season and entered into the teaching profession full time, starting out at Bonnie Doon Composite High School in the city where he had become a CFL super star, Edmonton.

"John Bright's strengths as an educator were the same strengths that he had used so successfully on the gridiron," wrote Warrick Lee Barrett. "He had tremendous stamina, a will to succeed and a burning enthusiasm for his job. What John brought consciously to the classroom that he left behind in the football arena was empathetic compassion." *(67)*

He eventually was promoted to vice principal and then principal. Due to his stature as a former football star and a leader in education circles, he was in demand as a speaker at various public functions and was adept at motivational speeches. He was also known for his unusual habit of writing letters to many of the students when they graduated from his class, offering heartfelt advice and wishing them well in the future.

Besides his heavy administration schedule, Bright managed to find time to coach basketball and football at a nearby senior high.

"I coach run-and-shoot, press all over the court, while the other guys sit in a zone," he told Maury White. "I never get in any problems up here because of race but I get criticized for coaching American-style basketball." *(68)*

Always seeking competition of some sort, he continued pitching softball, and enjoyed bowling and golf. He led the city bowlers in high average for three straight years.

John's ending was sudden and tragic in that he was still a relatively young man. Suffering from a knee injury that was probably a result of his many years of football, he decided to undergo an operation to get it fixed. He was scheduled for surgery at the University of Alberta Hospital on December 13, 1983, in Edmonton and died in the process of receiving anesthetics. The official cause of death was listed as a heart attack.

Friends, former teammates and fans were stunned when they heard the news. Longtime associates like Paul Morrison and Jim Zabel, a legendary Iowa sportscaster, were greatly saddened.

"We had corresponded through the years and it was always a delight to hear from him," said Morrison. "It was really shocking when he died at such a young age."

Zabel had been a student at the University of Iowa and was editor of the student newspaper when word arrived that Nile Kinnick had died at sea. In 2010, he said the word of Bright's death was almost as stunning. Though Bright was buried in Holy Cross Cemetery in Edmonton, a memorial service was held in Des Moines and Zabel was one of several to give eulogies.

During his very long career at WHO Radio, Zabel became friends with most of the top stars at Iowa, Iowa State, Drake and UNI. So where does he rate Johnny Bright?

"I feel he was the best football player to ever pull on a uniform in the state of Iowa," said Zabel. "His coach at Drake, Warren Gaer, told me Johnny would have been a great linebacker but he was too valuable as an offensive weapon to put on defense. He was big, strong, fast and a superb natural athlete. But beyond that, Johnny Bright was a great guy to talk to and hang out with. He was a hero to me, in life and in death." *(69)*

The memory of The Greatest Bulldog shines brightly across the lands where football is enjoyed and appreciated. He is a member of the Canadian Football League Hall of Fame, the Alberta (Canada) Sports Hall of Fame, the College Football Hall of Fame in South Bend, Indiana, the Des Moines Register Iowa Sports Hall of Fame, the Drake University Hall of Fame and the Iowa Fast-Pitch Softball Hall of Fame. His jersey (No. 43) is the only one to ever be retired at Drake, and his Edmonton jersey (No. 24) was retired by the Eskimos.

Drake has continued to honor its most famous athlete in numerous ways. In 1969 he was named the greatest football player in school history. But the ultimate tribute came in special ceremonies on September 30, 2006, when the field on which he once played so brilliantly was officially named Johnny Bright Field at Drake Stadium. Among the many who came to pay tribute were old teammates and members of his family. Game balls were given to his daughters who attended, Kandis Bright and Deanie Bright-Johnson.

"On behalf of the Bright family, we'd like to say thank you for a great honor toward the family," said his daughter, Kandis. "Our father had accomplished so many things in such a short lifetime and we in the family are extremely proud of every one of them. There couldn't be a better honor than to have our father's name here on the Drake field. It's fantastic."

"Johnny Bright was an immensely gifted athlete who gave his heart and his body to Drake University," read a statement from the Board of Trustees. "As an alumnus of Drake, he went on to a distinguished career as a football player in Canada, and – perhaps more important – as a gifted and highly-successful teacher and school administrator who had a positive impact on the lives of thousands of young people."

The National Association for Advancement of Colored People (NAACP) also had representatives at the ceremony and presented a plaque of appreciation to Drake.

"The NAACP is excited to present this award to the university because of Drake's respect for, and the mark of distinction that it has placed upon, Johnny Bright. Naming the field after one of the great African-American football players of our time will provide the opportunity for the Drake University community and the people of Iowa to learn about Johnny Bright and his great accomplishments not only in football but in the equal treatment of all people.

"Following a notable professional football career, Bright had a highly successful career in education as a teacher and administrator. By growing Johnny Bright's legend and continuing to recognize his accomplishments, we are able to bring his true combination of education and sport to public view, so that Johnny Bright can continue teaching others."

In 2006, Roger Capone, who played with Bright at Drake, sent a letter to Paul Morrison explaining that he had long ago written a letter advocating that the stadium be named for Bright. He also reminisced about his playing days with the

Triumph and Tragedy

This is how Fred Becker appeared in the summer of 1918 as a Marine officer in France. This portrait hangs inside American Legion Post 138, named for Lt. Becker and Lt. Carl Chapman, another casualty of World War I. The post is in Waterloo, the hometown of the two soldiers.

The entrance to East Waterloo High School displays a plaque in memory of Lt. Fred Becker and another classmate, Private Lynn E. Miller. The plaque (pictured above) is to the right of the flagpole in front of the balcony. It was a gift from the Class of 1920.

Special Photo Section

Johnny Bright was featured on several card sets sold in Canada. In the Post card (above), the written description is in two languages, English and French. The Wheaties card (right) can bring as much as $200 in top shape.

The Nile Kinnick card below was produced as part of the legendary All-American series in 1955. Note that his first name is misspelled.

This round chip featuring the image of Johnny Bright was produced in 1956 by Humpty Dumpty Potato Chip Company.

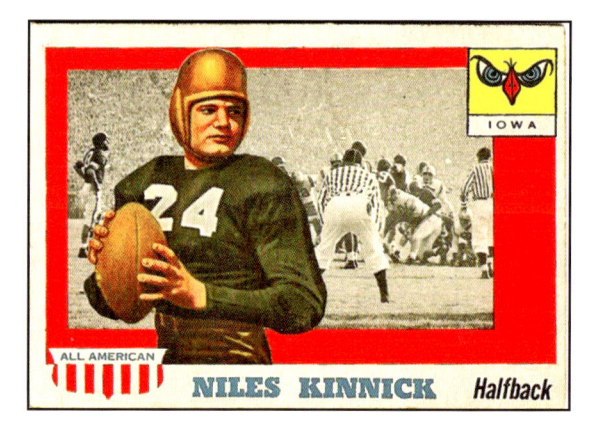

Special Photo Section

In 1939, Nile Kinnick was the toast of the sporting nation. He led the courageous Hawkeye team known as "The Ironmen" to wins over national powers and won the Heisman Trophy as the country's top college football player. His jersey, No. 24, is one of just two that has been retired by the University of Iowa.

A larger-than-life statue of Iowa's greatest athletic hero greets fans who come to Kinnick Stadium each fall in Iowa City. The 12 foot statue, by Lawrence J. Nowlan, of Cornish, New Hampshire, stands on a four-foot tall base covered in mosabi black granite and is located in the Krause Family Plaza.

Triumph and Tragedy

Jack Trice's name greets fans at the east entrance of the stadium where the Cyclones play each fall. It is the only Division I football stadium in the nation named for an African-American.

The Drake Bulldogs play football on a field named for its brightest star, surrounded by a track named for the legendary announcer Jim Duncan. Johnny Bright football field was dedicated on September 30, 2006.

Drake sensation.

"John never once complained to me about a missed block," wrote Capone. "Believe me, there were many of them. I was the left guard who had to pull out and lead the running and take out the defensive end. More times than not, the only way I could get the block was to throw my body (cross body) and hope that I could at least slow him down. John did the rest.

"Even though I have had two hip replacements, I have no regrets for I feel honored to have played with such a complete athlete and sportsman. John always respectfully called me Ol' Man. I called him friend." *(70)*

Central High, Bright's old school in Fort Wayne, closed in 1971 and now houses the school district's adult education center. There is no mention of Bright anywhere in the building, according to an official at the facility.

However, Edmonton has not forgotten its famous athlete and educator. In May of 2009, it was announced that Edmonton was naming one of six new schools after Bright. The schools were designed to accommodate 850 students, from grades kindergarten through ninth. Bev Esslinger, school board president, said the goal was to name the schools after people who had made a lasting impact on public education.

"People who have inspired others for generations are who we are looking for," she added. Of course, Johnny Bright was the perfect fit for such an honor. He had spent his entire life - from the moment he arrived at Drake University in 1948 to that fateful day in 1983 when he entered the hospital - trying to inspire others with his athletic feats, his modesty, his sportsmanship and his passion for growth.

On a web site, a Canadian fan named Robert Harrison wrote a moving tribute to Bright several years ago.

"Growing up in Canada as a fan of our brand of football, Johnny Bright is one of those greats many of us living here came to appreciate and admire for their skill and tenacity on the field as well as off it through their contributions to the communities where they played and later worked and raised families in. While Canada is by no means perfect in terms of racial tolerance and harmony, many African-American athletes like Mr. Bright were able to find a place where they could work, raise a family and live in safety and relative serenity, building friendships and establishing roots in many cities across Canada.

"There are many examples of men like Johnny Bright who came to Canada and established themselves as leaders of their newfound communities, enriching the lives of many of their neighbors. In my hometown, a gentleman by the name of George Reed came here to play professional football and, like Mr. Bright, became a pillar in the community (he also managed to break many of Mr. Bright's CFL rushing records!). Mr. Reed probably said it best while accepting an award for community service many years ago: 'I came …. I played …. I stayed.'

"It's a shame that many American communities were unable to benefit from the example and leadership exhibited by Johnny Bright, George Reed and many others. But as they say, 'your loss was our gain' in this case."

Like Nile Kinnick and Jack Trice before him, Johnny Bright has been immortalized by the school that he served so gallantly. His memory lives on in Des Moines, Iowa, and Edmonton, Canada, as students of all ages continue their educational journeys. It is a legacy that would have made Johnny Bright smile once again.

Epilogue

There is an infinite string of events that winds through time and connects all the happenings, in some way or another. Nearly all events are of a nature that they leave no impression whatsoever, and simply pass from consciousness as soon as they are over. Other events, however, endure for centuries or, even, millennia.

Time itself consists of a never-ending parade of men and women, known and unknown, moving along at their own pace, from day to day and week to week and year to year in the only fashion they know.

The moments that stand out in the collective memory we call history. History is what we remember of memorable men and women, and the events in which they participated, and what we choose to make of the events that transpired. And, of course, what we decide is worthy of writing down.

What we often forget in telling stories of those who came before us is that they were, in the final evaluation, people just like you and me, with hopes and dreams and strengths and weaknesses. They lived and loved, fought and rested, dreamed and hoped, just like us.

And that is true of the four men whose lives are now connected through the pages of this book. Their days on earth overlapped, from one to the other, starting with Fred Becker and ending with Johnny Bright. And their stories are intertwined by the fact that they came to the public's attention within the boundaries of an area we know as Iowa.

Fred Becker was born on November 6, 1895, earned his fame in Iowa City, and died on July 18, 1918, in France. Jack Trice was born in 1902, earned his fame in Ames, and died there on October 8, 1923.

Nile Kinnick was born in Adel, Iowa, on July 9, 1918, and became the greatest Hawkeye of them all before dying on June 2, 1943, in the waters off the coast of Venezuela. Johnny Bright was born on June 11, 1930, in Fort Wayne, Indiana, but earned his fame at Drake University in Des Moines, before moving on to even greater glory in Edmonton, Canada. He died there on December 14,

1983.

The string of these four lives began, therefore, in 1895 in Waterloo and expired in 1983, in Edmonton, Canada.

For many years, I have felt a sense of irony that the day of Nile's death combines my birth date with that of my wife. Bev was born on June 2 of 1947, and I was born in 1943! Furthermore, Fred Becker was born only several blocks from where my father grew up in Waterloo, and we attended the same high school. The Johnny Bright Incident occurred on my birthday, October 20. So far, I have not found any connection to Jack Trice other than my grandmother once told me that the Chapman clan came to Iowa from Ohio, where Jack was born and raised.
I make nothing of these facts other than the dates have combined to make themselves stand out in my mind.

All four men had lives that combined triumph and tragedy. The purpose of this book is to tell their stories to a new generation of Iowans so that they may continue to endure in written form for future generations of Iowans, and for Americans who love history and respect the lives of those who came before them.

The accomplishments of Fred Becker, Jack Trice, Nile Kinnick and Johnny Bright deserve to keep being told and retold. That is the ultimate goal of a book like this.

Footnotes

1. *75 Years With the Fighting Hawkeyes*, page 58.
2. Ibid, page 60.
3. Ibid, page 62.
4. *All Quiet on the Western Front*, pages 12, 13.
5. Ibid, page 133.
6. Ibid, pages 282, 283.
7. C-Span's Book Talk, May 25, 2008.
8. Black Hawk Country Biography. Transcribed by Sharyl Ferrall, posted 7/18/2004, source: Official Register, State of Iowa, 1921-22, Twenty-ninth number, Military decorations of Iowans in the World War, page 361.
9. Wikipedia, Alvin York.
10. *All Quiet on the Western Front*, page 88.
11. Ibid, page 234.
12. C-Span's Book Talk, April 29, 2008.
13. Waterloo Courier, 150-year anniversary issue of the Waterloo Courier, May 30, 2004, story by Pat Kinney, page 34.
14. Iowa State Parks Library, Jack Trice Collection.
15. *Football's Fallen Hero*, page 21.
16. Ibid, page 44.
17. Internet story.
18. Interview on Dec. 4, 1973, by Bill Walsh, for a paper now in the Iowa State Parks Library, Jack Trice Collection.
19. Iowa State Parks Library, Jack Trice Collection.
20. Ibid.
21. Interview by Gary Stowe on July 29, 1974, for a paper now in the Iowa State Parks Library, Jack Trice Collection.
22. Interview on Dec. 4, 1973, by Bill Walsh, for a paper now in the Iowa State Parks Library, Jack Trice Collection.
23. Matt Blair phone conversation, November 2009.
24. Nile Kinnick and the Ironmen, 60th Anniversary Special, Iowa City Press Citizen.
25. *Kinnick: The Man and the Legend*, page 12.
26. Ibid, page 26.
27. Ibid, page 24.
28. Nile Clarke Kinnick: A father's untold story of life with his famous son, Des Moines Sunday Register, August 6, 1989, page 13D.
29. *Kinnick: The Man and the Legend*, page 24.
30. *My Greatest Day in Football*, by Murray Goodman and Leonard Lewin, A.S. Barnes and Company, New York, 1948, page 11.
31. Undated DM Register article by Ron Maly.
32. Ronald Reagan quotes, personal interview in 1990 by Mike Chapman.

33. *A Hero Perished: The Diary & Selected Letters of Nile Kinnick*, pages 138-139.
34. Phone interview in 2009 with author.
35. Personal interview in 2003 with Peg Nelson by author.
36. *Kinnick: The Man and the Legend*, page 86.
37. Personal interview with Dr. James Van Allen in his office, by author.
38. *Kinnick: The Man and the Legend*, page 118.
39. *The Ironmen*, page xi.
40. *Kinnick: The Man and the Legend*, page 117.
41. John Carlson column, Des Moines Register, Sunday, January 25, 2003, pages 1A and 20A.
42. *Johnny Bright, Champion*, by Warrick Lee Barrett, Commonwealth Publications, 1996.
43. Des Moines Sunday Register, story by Maury White, March 29, 1970, 1-S
44. Ibid, page 4-S.
45. Jim McGrew interview with author in June, 2009.
46. Des Moines Sunday Register, story by Maury White, March 29, 1970, 1-S.
47. Drake Quax 1952, yearbook, page 186.
48. Comments delivered by Paul Morrison on August 6, 2008, on the history of Drake football Ibid (page 181).
49. Drake Quax 1952, yearbook, page 186.
50. Blair Kerkhoff of the Kansas City Star in a 2000 article.
51. Jack Jennett phone interview with author on May 3, 2010.
52. Drake Quax 1952, yearbook, page 190.
53. Paul Morrison interview with author in April 18, 2010.
54. Jack Jennett phone interview with author on May 3, 2010.
55. Robert Ray phone interview with author on May 3, 2010.
56. Paul Morrison interview with author on April 18, 2010.
57. The News-Sentinel, Fort Wayne, Ind., "Johnny Bright Gets His Day," column by Blake Sebring, Sept. 28, 2006, Quoting Des Moines Register article from 1980.
58. Fort Wayne (Indiana) News-Sentinel, column by Blake Sebring, "Johnny Bright Finally Gets His day," September 28, 2006.
59. Blair Kerkhoff in the Kansas City Star, Oct. 21, 2001, D-1.
60. Los Angeles Times, Oct. 21, 2001, "Photos Taught A Lesson," by Adam Buckley Cohen.
61. Fort Wayne (Indiana) News-Sentinel, column by Blake Sebring, "Johnny Bright FinallyGets His day," September 28, 2006.
62. Barrett book, pages 86-92.
63. The Star Weekly Magazine, Sept. 28, 1957, article by Jim Hunt.
64. Bud Grant phone interview with author May 3, 2010.
65. Jim Walden phone interview with author May 10, 2010.
66. Des Moines Register article, by Tony Cordaro, July 3, 1957.
67. Barrett book, page 102.
68. Des Moines Sunday Register, story by Maury White, March 29, 1970.
69. Jim Zabel phone interview with author May 2, 2010.
70. Roger Capone email to Paul Morrison, 2006.

Bibliography

1. *All Quiet on the Western Front*, by Erich Maria Remarque, translated by A. W. Wheen, Little Brown and Company, Boston, 38th printing, 1958.
2. *Hawkeye Legends*, Lists & Lore, by Mike Finn and Chad Leistikow, Sports Publishing, Inc., Champaign, Illinois, 1998.
3. *A Hero Perished: The Diary & Selected Letters of Nile Kinnick*, edited by Paul Baender, University of Iowa Press, Iowa City, 1991.
4. *The Ironmen: The 1939 Hawkeyes*, by Scott M. Fisher, Media Publishing, Lincoln, Nebraska, 1989.
5. *Kinnick: The Man and the Legend*, by D. W. Stump, The University of Iowa, Iowa City, 1975.
6. *75 Years With The Fighting Hawkeyes*, by Dick Lamb and Bert McGrane, The University of Iowa Athletic Department, Iowa City, Iowa, 1964.
7. *Football's Fallen Hero*, by Steven L. Jones, Cover to Cover Books, Perfection Learning Corporation, Logan, Iowa, 2000.
8. Nile Kinnick and the Ironmen, *60th Anniversary Special*, Iowa City-Press Citizen, Iowa City, August 28, 1999.
9. *My Greatest Day in Football*, by Murray Goodman and Leonard Lewin, A.S. Barnes and Company, New York, 1948.
10. *Adel Living* magazine, February 8, 2003.
11. Nile Kinnick and the Ironmen, *60th Anniversary Special*, Iowa City-Press Citizen, Iowa City, August 28, 1999.
12. *Johnny Bright, Champion,* by Warrick Lee Barrett, M.D., to Excel publishing, San Jose, New York, Lincoln, 1996.
13. *Iowa History Journal* magazine, issues 1 to 5, 2009.

About The Author

Mike Chapman has been writing biographies for more than two decades. Among his 22 published books are *From Gotch to Gable: A History of Iowa Wrestling* (University of Iowa Press, 1981), *Iowans of Impact* (Enterprise Publishing, 1984), and *The Life and Legacy of Frank Gotch* (Paladin Press, 2007). A native of Waterloo, Iowa, Mr. Chapman retired from a 35-year newspaper career in 2002, his last position being publisher of the Newton Daily News. A native of Waterloo, Iowa, he and his wife, Bev, live in Newton, and publish the magazine *Iowa History Journal*.

www.mike-chapman.com
www.iowahistoryjournal.com